THE
CRITICAL
SECOND PHASE
OF YOUR
PROFESSIONAL
LIFE

THE
CRITICAL
SECOND PHASE
OF YOUR
PROFESSIONAL
LIFE

KEYS TO SUCCESS FOR AGE 40 AND BEYOND

ROBERT L. DILENSCHNEIDER

CITADEL PRESS
KENSINGTON PUBLISHING CORP.
www.kensingtonbooks.com

CITADEL PRESS books are published by

Kensington Publishing Corp.
850 Third Avenue
New York, NY 10022

All Kensington titles, imprints, and distributed lines are available at special quantity discounts for bulk purchases for sales promotions, premiums, fund raising, educational, or institutional use. Special book excerpts or customized printings can also be created to fit specific needs. For details, write or phone the office of the Kensington special sales manager: Kensington Publishing Corp., 850 Third Avenue, New York, NY 10022, attn: Special Sales Department, phone 1-800-221-2647.

Kensington and the K logo Reg. U.S. Pat. & TM Office
Citadel Press is a trademark of Kensington Publishing Corp.

First printing 2000

10 9 8 7 6 5 4 3 2 1

Printed in the United States of America

Library of Congress Cataloging-in-Publication Data

Dilenschneider, Robert L.
    The critical second phase of your professional life / keys to success for age 40 and beyond / Robert L. Dilenschneider.
        p.   cm.
    ISBN 1-55972-509-5 (hc)
    1. Career changes.   2. Middle aged persons—Employment.   3. Career development.   4. Professional employees.   I. Title.   II. Title: Critical 2nd phase of your professional life.
HF5384.D545   1999
650.14—dc21
                                                        99-23287
                                                        CIP

To Jack, Marti, and Mary
whose wisdom, guidance, and knowledge
made much of this possible.

CONTENTS

FOREWORD

by Ken Dychtwald

Ken Dychtwald, Ph.D., is the founder, president, and chief executive officer of Age Wave, LLC., in Emeryville, California. He's the author of *Bodymind, Healthy Aging,* and *Age Wave.* He has been featured in *Newsweek, Time, Fortune, BusinessWeek,* the *New York Times* and *Model Healthcare,* as well as on numerous television programs.

If you're over forty and experiencing a career shock—or several of them—you're right on schedule. Demographic trends have made careers for older workers very different than they were for Perry Mason, Marcus Welby, or Ward Cleaver. All Mason, Welby, and Cleaver had to do was their work. Your generation has to go through the rite of passage of getting fired, continuing to retool your skills, and managing the two, three, or four careers you'll have before you retire. In a global economy, organizations don't have the time to look out for your career. Welcome to the world of being a free agent.

There are three interrelated demographic trends that have revolutionized work life. The first is the shrinkage of the number of young adults available to work. At the end of this decade there will be nine million fewer eighteen- to thirty-four-year-olds than there were at the beginning of the decade, which means that older workers will increasingly bridge the labor gap by having longer careers. Our contemporaries are already doing some of the work younger people used to do: Retired computer programmers have been hired to prevent computers from going haywire at the end of the millennium; supermarkets and other retail establishments have created flexible part-time jobs for older workers. On the turnpikes, older workers take tolls. John Glenn served as a space shuttle payload specialist at seventy-seven.

The second trend is that a large portion of the workforce is becoming middle-aged. The majority of the seventy-six million baby-boomers are now over forty. Also, many members of the "Silent Generation" are still in the workforce. Because there are so many of them it's hard for older workers to get ahead today. Frustrated baby boomers, blocked from promotions or from becoming the boss, are leaving organizations and becoming freelancers or entrepreneurs. At forty-eight or fifty-two, they have realized that they don't want to do what they've been doing for fifteen more years. From their frustration has come a new ability to take a risk, sometimes even to start another career. I can't imagine Mason, Welby, or Cleaver ever changing careers.

At the same time demographics are crowding them, this massive group of middle-aged workers is also being affected by downsizing and mergers. In this new environment, many jobs have disappeared. One professional is now expected to do the jobs of several. Rather than a setup with a manager and three workers, there might just be two workers, period. Because older workers usually make more than younger workers, they are frequently the first to get the axe. After this kind of career shock, many middle-aged professionals are forced to refocus and to take control of their careers—which is what this book is about. The "powers that be" can no longer be trusted to take care of us. We need to fend for ourselves.

The third trend is that "old age," as we've known it, is gone. People are healthier, and a growing number want to work as long as they can—right into their eighties and nineties. Recent polls sponsored by the American Association of Retired Persons (AARP) and the National Council on Aging found that 40 percent of retired people would rather be working. People are taking early retirement, moving to retirement communities, and then moving back to a metropolitan area to work. Working is now recognized as a life force.

Longer careers might become the norm—especially with Social Security being so precarious. There's talk in Congress about extending the retirement age to seventy or older.

Older workers need to learn to define *work* broadly. It doesn't have to mean an eight-, ten-, or twelve-hour day at one desk at one company. Work might mean temporary assignments at several companies, a part-time job telecommuting from a computer at home, or even volunteering.

Given that careers will continue to be longer and multiple careers will become more common, sabbaticals and extended breaks from work will likely become routine. Professionals will be able to enter, leave, and reenter the workforce without stigma. Workers will have several "time-outs" to rethink their professional goals. The present trend toward simplification can help professionals reduce their expenses so they have the financial resources to enable them to take time off for extended periods of time.

There will also be many late bloomers among those with a lifetime of several careers. The man who gets his master's degree in social work at sixty might turn out to be a brilliant therapist. His previous careers might have been mediocre, but now he's found his niche. Goethe completed *Faust* when he was over eighty. Michelangelo started working on St. Peter's when he was seventy-one. Professionals in their fifties, sixties, seventies, and eighties will be making significant accomplishments.

In college, you anticipated a linear career path. You would climb the ladder in one company. You would identify yourself as "an engineer at General Electric." You would be loyal, and your company would be loyal in return. Then you would retire. But now, all the rules have changed. Now you have more than one career. In your professional lifetime, you might be a lawyer, a manager of a start-up company, an executive director of an animal-rescue organization, and an Amway salesperson. You no longer want to climb the ladder as much; you want to remain *marketable*. So, in your present job, you gravitate toward those assignments that teach you hot skills. As a perk, you're getting more and more training. The new mentality is that whether you work for Ford or are an entrepreneur, you're ultimately working for yourself.

Every professional is a free agent. Your loyalty is to *yourself*, and once you have put the kids through college and paid for a few weddings, you can "afford" to have fun working. You can be a park ranger for minimum wage or do extensive volunteer work.

Some of you might find yourselves as part of the "wisdom department" in a particular company, or a "wisdom consultant" for several companies, where you'll use your experience to help guide organizations from making the same old mistakes. If we had "wisdom departments" during the heyday of reengineering, there might have been more common sense in reconfiguring work.

Increasingly, work will be divided up into packages that a seventy- or eighty-year-old can do. It will be okay to be confused. The so-called midlife crisis will become midlife and later-life crises. To deal with these new shocks, professionals will have to approach their careers in radically different ways. Careers won't unfold, they'll be engineered. Setbacks, rather than being embarrassments, will be opportunities to try things a different way. There will be less urgency to achieve some grandiose goal by the time you're thirty-eight. Multiple careers mean second, third, and fourth chances to "make it big," and organizations that keep score of our careers, such as the business media, will have to see professionals as works in progress. The chief executive officer who lost a job at fifty-two is in transition. There will be many George Foremans, John Travoltas, and Donald Trumps with the ability and drive to enjoy comebacks.

The careers you'll enter in maturity can initially be shocking, but once you have adjusted, good things will be ahead. Those who are aging will be the most powerful group in society and the workplace, and if you use your power right you can change policies there. You can certainly change them through legislation.

To manage your new careers you'll need new mind-sets and new strategies. *The Critical Second Phase of Your Professional Life* introduces those mind-sets and provides a new kind of toolbox. It probably won't make career shocks less painful, but it can make those crises produc-tive in bringing you from where you are to where you need to be.

ACKNOWLEDGMENTS

While putting together this book, I received generous support from many different sources.

The Critical Second Phase of Your Professional Life would not have been possible without the able assistance of Mary Jane Genova. Ms. Genova helped conceptualize the ideas, conduct the research, and prepare what you have read here. All of us—particularly the author—are in her debt.

This book also would not have been possible without the support and encouragement of my wife, Jan, and my sons Geoffrey and Peter, who exhibited boundless patience and endured long suffering as I moved this project forward. All three contributed ideas and suggestions that helped add richness to my work.

Reid Boates, my agent, gave me the inspiration to write the book and to undertake still others in the future. Without his encouragement, this volume would not have been possible.

I am, of course, indebted to Carol Publishing chieftain Steven Schragis who gave me the opportunity to address the needs of those men and women at the middle, or end, of their careers; and to senior editor Francine Hornberger, who offered valued assistance in putting all the pieces together.

As to the substance of the book, I wish to thank everyone who agreed to be interviewed. Dr. Ken Dychtwald, one of the world's acknowledged experts on working with, and benefiting from the skills and abilities of older people, was outstanding. Bob Stone, who has worked with me since the late 1970s and who has a special appreciation of seasoned professionals in the marketplace, was simply incredible. Cathleen Black, who has embraced several careers, all successful, and now leads the parade for Hearst Magazines, made an enormous contribution as did John Thompson, who shared with me his invaluable insights about the field of interim placement.

The list of those who provided assistance is long and illustrious. As always, Rick Taylor, head of one of the top executive search firms in the country, who has worked with dozens in the age category I deal with, was singularly insightful in his observations, as was Dr. Patricia Cardinale, a leading authority on the motivations, concerns, and goals of individuals in this age group, who made comments that were right on the mark. Carol Kinsey Goman, who has written many books in her own right and who is a consummate professional in communications, added her particular expertise to this volume as did Steve Harrison, who leads one of the premier out-placement firms in the world, Lee Hecht Harrison, and is also a great friend.

Jack O'Dwyer, a leading expert in my own field, rendered needed objectivity that was without parallel. Dr. Richard Brockman, himself a bestselling author, created a dimension for the book that is quite special and deserves high praise; and James Scofield O'Rourke, IV, one of the pre-eminent business school professors in the country, who happens to teach at my alma mater, Notre Dame, likewise brought a unique perspective to the subject.

Once again, John Kasic, from the Dilenschneider Group, provided his usual extraordinary support to bring this book to fruition.

Finally, this book and all my other previous works and, indeed, my career would not have been possible without the able assistance of Joan Avagliano, to whom I owe much.

THE CRITICAL SECOND PHASE OF YOUR PROFESSIONAL LIFE

INTRODUCTION

There was a very profound sadness. It ends with a whimper, not a bang.

—Man in his forties laid off from Wall Street

NO MORE GOLDEN BOYS AND GIRLS

Career shock wasn't supposed to happen to us. We were among the brightest and the best. We learned to avoid the pitfalls that killed other careers. Frequently, our wisdom was quoted in the media. People said we had the Midas touch. Then we got older...

Recently, the front page of the *Wall Street Journal* carried a story about managers in their fifties who had been out of work during the recession of the early 1990s. But when the economy bounced back, they didn't get comparable jobs. The boom passed them by.[1]

WHAT DO I DO?

Almost every day, people my age and older call me. They are chief executive officers (CEOs), and other senior executives, managers, and even those from nonprofits. They flat-out ask: "What do I do?" These men and women are in their forties through their seventies and are facing radical changes in their work lives and careers. They're scared. They've always been on top of things and don't feel on top of things now. The world of work, where they were once so comfortable, has become a threatening place for them.

3

They blame their age. They're probably right. For some careers, advancing age sounds the death knell. For other careers, though, age is a plus. I blossomed when I was fifty. I set up my own business. I broke all the rules of "good management." I also became a father. But the decade leading up to the big-five-oh was the most confusing time of my life. This book is one I wish I had had in my forties.

CAREER SHOCKS

A CEO called me because he was being forced to retire. He wondered if he should move to Florida or try to find another company to run. His health was good and he wanted to work, but he wondered who would hire him. Although the prospect may appear to be remote for someone like himself, he is still haunted by the image of a man his age who bags groceries at the supermarket. Will he wind up that way?

Another CEO was told to turn his company around in eighteen months. Can he pull it off, or should he cry "Uncle" and surrender to the fact that he no longer has that old fire in the belly? Could he resign and teach courses in a business school—or maybe start a small company? At sixty-three, he doesn't feel like he has another turn-around in him.

One senior executive who contacted me had been passed over for a promotion and wondered what her next step should be. She wanted to try to launch a marketing consulting firm, but she never envisioned going out on her own at fifty-eight years of age. *That's almost sixty.*

A manager on Wall Street called to tell me that he was let go. Just like that. Within two hours, a ten-year career went out the window. He wondered if he is too old to get another job on Wall Street. He doesn't know what else he can do to earn six figures.

The fifty-year-old head of a nonprofit organization sent out fifty résumés, but she did not get even one bite. She used to be a hot ticket. She wondered if it's her age. Should she just focus on keeping the job she has?

THERE ARE A LOT OF US

"What should I do?" Many people over forty are asking that question about their work lives. We'll have plenty of company. According to

HR Magazine, in twenty years, more than one-third of all workers will be fifty years of age or older.[2] There is already a lot of gray hair on the commuter trains into Manhattan. In the *AARP Bulletin*, Robert Lewis pointed out that the national trend toward early retirement bottomed out in 1985. A growing number of the seventy-six million baby boomers indicated that they want to work as long as possible.[3] Too many of us have watched our colleagues go off into retirement—and be miserable. Our mantra seems to be, "I'll work 'til I drop." Seventy-nine-year-old Bob Stone, who works on my staff, believes it would be a privilege to die at his desk.

A MAN IN FULL

This issue of aging has also found its way into the arts. In Tom Wolfe's novel, *A Man in Full*, sixty-year-old Charlie Croker, like us, also wonders what he should do. His financial empire is on the verge of collapse. His knee is bothering him. And his family treats him like a child.[4]

Wolfe's books, such as *Bonfire of the Vanities*, have always been about major social trends. In the 1980s, that social trend was greed and arrogance on Wall Street. Today, as depicted in *A Man in Full*, that social trend is about the older professional trying to find his place in a new world of work. Croker can be pretty dense, but even he realizes, "Nobody wants to hear war stories from a sixty-year-old man."[5] Eventually, he sees that what he has to do is reassess just about everything in his life and make some changes.

WE'RE PIONEERS!

"What do we do?" There are no easy answers. That's because we are the first to be hit by the "Age Assault." We are seventy-six million baby boomers and millions more from the Silent Generation. We are pioneers in trying to stay employable after forty. And the next generations are watching us.

You might say that we are all participating in a gigantic experiment about how older professionals can keep earning money. We're not dummies. We know that there is definitely prejudice out there against older workers. A study in the hospitality industry, for example, found that younger workers felt that older workers are more difficult to supervise.[6] I know of thousands of professionals in their fifties who put their college graduation date on their résumés—and never received one reply. I ran focus groups of young professionals who say that older workers are set in their ways and don't understand or utilize technology—that they grab for the phone, not for e-mail.

WINNERS AND LOSERS

In this book, I share what I've learned over the past fifteen years about this experiment—what's working for us and what isn't, and the new elite of winners and losers among older workers.

What are winners doing that the losers are not? Plenty. I talked to the winners. I interviewed experts in everything from executive search firms to psychotherapy. I talked with families of those our age. There are plenty of books, both pop and serious, about aging in general and I read them. I considered the optimism of Letty Cottin Pogrebin in *Getting Over Getting Older*[7] and the pessimism of Betty Friedan's *The Fountain of Age*.[8] I asked myself why there aren't more Katharine Grahams who blossom in middle age. Why couldn't Watergate reporter Carl Bernstein, who became world-famous at 28, sustain the heights in his later career? Does talk-show host Larry King keep getting better because of his age?

WHAT I'VE FOUND OUT

In my search I found a number of surprising things, including:

- Older people who keep working, despite layoffs and losing their businesses, don't think a lot about their age. They acknowledge it as a fact, like having blue eyes, and then focus on keeping the powers that be and clients looking good. That person they make look good may be twenty years younger than they are. Winners operate age neutral. The converse is also true. Those who are preoccupied with age wind up being preoccupied with themselves. They become a closed system and can't keep their eye on the ball.

- Successful older professionals have developed efficient ways of keeping up-to-date on everything from music to the Internet.

Some of them use their own children as guides, others figure out what media to monitor. They also waste little time judging trends. They leave that to people like George Will, who get paid for being critical of society.

- Older winners in the work world realize that determination can sometimes be a curse. Rather than fixing solely on getting a good job, they hang loose and are also open to temp work and self-employment. One determined man spent two years trying to get a $60,000 job and lost his marriage in the process. The job he finally did get didn't work out. He was too eager to please and got on everyone's nerves.

- Successful people have backup careers. For years a man I'll call Sam worked in MIS at a consumer-products company, but he always kept up with his brother's funeral business. When his company was bought, Sam had the choice of going to work with his brother or looking for another computer job. Having that choice kept him from becoming desperate. Even when things are going well, older winners will be picking up a real estate license or working weekends in another field. They realize that tomorrow they can wake up and the demand for their expertise could have vanished.

- All work and no play make Jack and Jill unemployable. Experts in executive search report that hobbies make a person come across as fully engaged in life. Work robots come across as "old." Connecting through networks frequently involves exploiting similar outside interests—perhaps you belong to the same athletic club or you both fly jets for fun. One middle-aged real estate broker got a major listing because, just like the seller, she was interested in animal rescue.

- The biggest gold mine for interests is our own family. That mix of generations keeps us informed about every stage of life. And families are powerful support systems when tough times come. It's never too late to reconnect with the family.

- Professionals who are able to keep making revenue know who they are. In these volatile times, self-awareness helps us make the right moves for ourselves. In many situations today there are no longer right and wrong answers, per se. There are just answers that are right or wrong for us. When we know ourselves we can ignore conventional wisdom and take smart risks. Members of the Iacocca team who came to Chrysler from Ford left good jobs in their forties and fifties to form a near-bankrupt company—and they became millionaires and celebrities. Had they stayed at Ford they would probably have been stuck in middle management. They were sure about who they were.

- Whether ministers or psychotherapists, winners get help when they're overwhelmed. One fifty-four-year-old vendor I work with was being overworked by a large client. The situation became so bad that she considered "firing" the client. She had five sessions with a clinical social worker/therapist and saw that she had choices: fire the client, phase out the client, talk things over with the client, get other clients to replace that one, or retire. She decided to talk things over with the client. She and the therapist role-played what she should say and how she should say it. Things worked out fine. Professionals who turn only to themselves for help are likely to get caught in a depression, the emotional common cold of the aging professional. Depression comes from isolation.

- Those who survive recognize that values aren't forever. At forty, we may want to still be all work. At fifty, our values may soften and we'll want to make a difference in society. If we don't heed those changes in our values, we'll be making poor choices.

- Winners take proper pride in their past and the past of the company. Today, the cliché is to "move on," but to go forward we often have to understand our past. Some of us, including myself, are investigating and writing family histories.

- Winners create their own status systems. They're not afraid to say good-bye forever to a large brand-name corporation to work at a company of five hundred—or even fifty—people. Recently, the *New York Times Magazine* did a special issue on status symbols. In America, status symbols change as often as hemlines. Given that, we might as well be in charge of what our own status symbols will be.[9]

IT ALL STARTS WITH A QUESTION

Gaining all this insight usually starts out with one question—What do I do? And more often than not, it's asked while feeling plenty of mental anguish. Learning to survive as an older worker is a hard-won victory, but it's worth every bit of the pain. I wouldn't trade the professional—and person—I am now for the hard-charger I was at thirty.

AGE—A PROBLEM TO SOLVE

In my fifteen years looking at this issue from all sides, I've discovered that age isn't a demon that possesses our body. Our age is simply another professional problem to solve. Remember when we had to learn how to use the personal computer? At the time, that challenge seemed like the end of the world. But we did learn and moved on to other problems. Age is the same thing. It can hit us in the stomach, but once we deal with it, it can be smooth sailing. Once my colleagues are past the pain, they and their clients tell me they've never had a happier time in their careers.

Now You Know...

- If you're aging, you're not alone in the workplace. There are millions of us. So don't isolate yourself.
- Winners in the age game are age neutral.
- Initially, aging can cause career shock.
- Aging is a problem to be solved.

I

WHY WE COME ACROSS AS "OLD"

I think of coworkers and bosses as 'old' when they're not trusting of new ideas or new approaches. They've been doing something for ten years and they don't want to try something different.
> —Twenty-something member of a focus group, New York, 1998

What Do I Do?

- Every other worker here my age has gotten the axe.
- I'm out of the loop. I know it's because people think of me as old.
- One day I'm a "golden boy." The next I'm treated like a has-been.
- I want to come across as younger.
- No one told me that age was going to deep-six my career.

"OLD" IS HOW PEOPLE PERCEIVE US

There's a lot of confusion about age and about being labeled old. But there's no necessary correlation between our age and others treating us as old. People only treat us as old if they see us acting "old." It may have nothing to do with our chronological age. We have no control over our age. But we do have control over our behavior.

I may be fifty, sixty, or seventy, but that can be irrelevant to how people treat me. If I still accomplish a great deal, people in their twenties and thirties will treat me as a valued colleague. They will return my calls right away. They will listen to what I have to say. If they disagree with me, they'll give me candid feedback. In short, they will continue to take me seriously. My age is a fact of life that may have very little to do with how I function at work.

On the other hand, I may be forty and resist working on teams. I may refuse to pay attention in the seminars on leadership. I may talk a lot at work about some personal medical problem. You can bet that I'll be written off as a has-been and will be gone in the next round of staff cuts. The powers that be will say, "This person is old. Let's get rid of the deadwood."

WHY WE'RE GETTING THE AXE

Many, if not most, of the chief executive officers of major corporations are over forty. IBM's Lou Gerstner is a dynamo. On snow days he's frequently the first one in. Ron Jensen, a senior executive, is running dozens of private financial service companies that affect tens of millions of people. Steve Jobs, still boyish-looking, but actually forty-four, just turned Apple around. At my firm, where half the staff is over fifty, there's no difference between the hours the older workers put in and those the younger ones do. Both groups have the same grueling travel schedules, and they all have to keep up with very demanding clients. My family and I have doctors, dentists, and household staff over forty.

Yet, it's our age group which has become the first to be let go— especially in *Fortune* 500 companies. Downsizing since the late 1980s put millions on the beach. In Fairfield County, Connecticut, there are neighborhoods full of homeowners who have been out of work for years.

Why are older workers being targeted to lose jobs? And once we're out, why does it take so many of us so long to regroup?

HIGH COMPENSATION

One part of the problem, says James Medoff in *U.S. News & World Report*, is that older workers tend to receive higher compensation than younger workers. Medoff studied personnel records and found that workers who have been on the payroll for ten years were receiving about 30 percent more than their colleagues, even though their performance reviews weren't better.[1]

This salary range can be a real problem if we are let go from our current jobs. When we interview for new jobs, we take our salary expectations with us. But this can be detrimental. Even though a smaller firm may hesitate to hire us because they don't think they can afford us, and despite myriad rejections by various firms, we still put that $75,000 salary figure down on the application. In chapter 4 and chapter 8, I discuss how we can exit this trap.

YOUTHFUL INDUSTRIES

The second reason older workers get canned so often is that in some industries it's just bad form to have older workers in the corporate culture.[2] They look wrong for the part. Peter Lynch can speak about investments, but at his age he wouldn't have much credibility discussing the latest music group. And can you imagine how well Bob Hope would be received as a spokesperson for Nike?

How many of us are willing to start over in another industry? In my chapter on getting smart, I discuss how common it is for people to retool by acquiring another body of knowledge.

GETTING STALE

A third reason we get hit is that we have fallen asleep at the wheel. We're oblivious to new trends and new approaches. We assume that these are "special situations" and that we can more or less coast through them. We don't notice that everything is changing around us. But by the time it catches up with us, there's usually no way to redeem ourselves. If we do make a comeback after we've been caught napping, it will probably not be with our current boss in our current job. My chapter on bosses explains that at any age, the ticket to survival is to learn how to handle the boss.

ACTING OLD

The fourth reason that older workers get let go is that they might be excellent in performance, but they shoot themselves in the foot by acting "old." They're the ones who groan about new software. They're critical of new magazines like *Wired* or *Swing*. They're the ones who make all the jokes about reengineering. They're too arrogant to be politically correct in the office. They're addicted to nostalgia, always referencing "the good old days."

Some people manage to grow older without seeming old. Madonna turned forty in 1998, but she has as much energy as she did at twenty. It was rumored that her biggest fear was getting old. Would people still have the same enthusiasm for her? Would she still be able to get away with her outrageous behavior if she started acting "old"?

Acting "old" sinks more careers than a lousy performance, political shoot-outs, or being in the wrong place at the wrong time.[3] Workers who act "old" are an embarrassment to the organization as well as a nuisance: They can't be depended upon to perform. Later in this chapter, I will discuss how this group—the old geezers—can reinvent themselves.

WHAT TO DO

First of all, we should celebrate the good news that the stigma surrounding aging has lifted some. There have been a proliferation of books, such as *Controversial Issues in Aging*, which take on and dispel myths about the aging process.[4] A 1997 survey by Maryland's Towson State University found that many employees had positive attitudes about older workers. However, the chief barrier to hiring older workers is that employers can't find older workers with the needed skill levels.

A MATTER OF PRESENTATION

Some people have a talent for presenting themselves as they want to be seen. The legendary Frank Sinatra was a master of image. He got fat, his voice faltered, but when he got onstage, all people saw was the kid from Hoboken. In a wheelchair, the late former governor George Wallace of Alabama kept changing his views on race so that he came across as in touch.

Research shows that how we live our lives can help us present ourselves as vital. The MacArthur Foundation Study of Successful

Aging found that our health, cognitive abilities, and interests are more important than our heredity in how we age. Just because our parents withdrew from life at sixty doesn't mean we have to.

THE CAREER SINKER

If you look around government, small business, nonprofits, the top layers of larger organizations, and even television, you see plenty of grey hair. Age *is* present in the workplace. Just think about members of the U.S. Senate, owners and employees of franchise operations, former Red Cross head Elizabeth Dole, Ted Turner, and Mike Wallace.

The core problem with finding suitable work or an appropriate business to run when we're over forty is that often our skills don't match what's needed. It's possible for our skills to become out of date overnight.

A presentation writer went from making six figures to almost zero overnight. That's because suddenly clients wanted the visuals for their presentations to be done via Microsoft's PowerPoint. The writer couldn't use that technology.

A psychotherapist was trained in the Freudian approach. She was oriented towards digging into people's backgrounds to find the source of their problems. Health maintenance organizations judged that approach to be too inefficient. Before the psychotherapist could be reimbursed by insurance companies, she needed to learn new methods.

A manager had been used to doing his job and only his job. Then teamwork became pervasive in the organization. The manager was clueless about how to operate as part of a team.

The other night I saw former President George Bush on *Larry King Live*. He had taken up parachuting—he was keeping himself engaged in life. Although he didn't look "young," he *acted* young. Senator John Glenn was smart about pushing to get back into space. That experience will take years off his own outlook and how others perceive him.

The laid-off professional who stays home and vegetates is less likely to get future employment. That person will soon become "old."[5] Redemption lies in getting out of the house and getting involved in life. I've noticed that among professionals who get new jobs, the quickest are usually the ones who have been doing some type of volunteer work.

BOB STONE—ROLE MODEL FOR THE EMPLOYED

How we present ourselves has to be wholistic, or integrated. You can't be a tiger at getting new business and then complain about the declining morals of youth. You can't introduce innovative ways to write the department's speeches and then make dated jokes about ethnic groups. Our colleagues see us as a composite of all we say and do. If we talk or act "old" in any of our mannerisms, we're going to be written off.

One of the best role models around for distracting people from thinking about his age is seventy-nine-year-old Bob Stone. Stone has worked in public relations for me for many years and intends never to retire. He never departs from his energetic persona. One time he went to the hospital for surgery and kept in constant touch with the office—except when he was under anesthesia. Everyone back at the office got the message: Stone was physically resilient. What Stone trades for coming across as energetic, of course, is his license to whine about his aches and pains. He knows that his image has to be integrated: He can't perform like a forty-year-old worker and fall asleep after lunch like an old geezer.

* * *

INTERVIEW WITH BOB STONE

RD: Bob, how long have you been working full time?

BS: About fifty years. Ten of them were on newspapers and forty in public relations.

RD: At what age did you start "feeling your age"?

BS: If by "feeling your age," you mean feeling old, then I have to honestly say that I haven't yet felt my age. When I work, I feel the same now as I felt thirty years ago.

RD: By every measure, Bob, you're a survivor. You've managed to still make an excellent living despite your age. How did you survive?

BS: Well, survival dictates that you know the rules of the game, that you play by those rules, and that you travel the high road. In that way, you do what you're supposed to do, but at the same time you're not violating your values. One of the quickest ways to burn out is to go against your values. If your values are being compromised, maybe it's time that you slowly and quietly look around for another home for yourself. And, if you don't have fun doing your job, you could be losing it and not realizing it.

RD: Bob, over and over in the office you say that your aim is to work smarter, not harder. At that point in our careers when our energy level might be lower but we have accumulated so much wisdom, that might be the way to go.

BS: It's common sense that all of us, no matter what age, should be searching for ways to work smarter, not harder. By working smarter, I mean that I can figure out a better way to do something than I originally thought about doing it. For example, here I am with fifty press releases to get out. I can have my associate spend a lot of time on it or I can call a service that shoots them out in seconds. For me, using a vendor is a smarter way to go because my associate is then free to do other more important work.

RD: Bob, I've found you to be a very loyal employee. Some say that loyalty on the job is dead. Do you think that being loyal has helped you survive fifty years in the work world?

BS: Yes and no. Loyalty is important on a job. I've always been loyal to the company's mission, the boss, and those I'm working with. I like being loyal because I like having personal relationships on the job. I feel that I have had a good understanding of the people with whom I've worked over the years, and they've appreciated that I was interested in them.

However, loyalty will only take you so far. In addition, in the new global economy, you need skills of *all* kinds. To illustrate, when the chips are down, in the office or in an industry, you not only have to have your job down cold, you also have to know what political moves to make. You learn that through experience. You learn to be alert to what ground rules are changing in the office.

RD: As you know, Bob, in our line of work there can sometimes be conflicts between your loyalty to the boss or a client and what you think is the right way to do a job. Have you ever experienced a conflict—and was your job ever in danger?

BS: In my work I've never encountered that kind of conflict. My ultimate loyalty is always to my principles—the values I described before. If a boss won't allow me to do a job the way I think it needs to be done, then it's part of my loyalty to that boss and to my own values to explain why I think that X task should be done in such and such a manner. I've never lost a job over this. It's important to understand your own values. In that way, you won't get chewed up by the workplace.

RD: Just one more thing on loyalty. Are you saying that part of loyalty is telling the truth, that if you're loyal to bosses, you owe them the truth?

BS: You got it. More people lose jobs because they don't tell the truth about how a project should be done. Then the project blows up and the powers that be are angry because information has been concealed. Loyalty equals truth. Of course, it pays to be diplomatic in how you convey the truth.

RD: A few businesspeople who own firms have come to me and asked if I hire account reps way past forty years old because older employees tend to be docile, they tend to comply. Do you think that's true?

BS: No. Maybe those particular businesspeople want compliant employees, so that's the kind they hire. When I'm screening candidates for jobs at this firm I look for initiative, fire in the belly, a willingness to question me. If we were to hire someone docile—no matter what their age—the clients wouldn't be getting fresh thinking.

RD: In every profession, we talk about current career goals. Do you have any career goals right now?

BS: You bet. My biggest career goal is to die right at my desk. When I die I want people to know that I was working at the time. Another big career goal is to always increase the contribution I'm making in the office. If I keep doing that I have a better shot at getting a good bonus. As you know, I'm always coming into your office and trying to find out how I can add value. When a company hires a public relations firm like ours, clients expect you to tell them how you can help them—not ask them what you can do for them. That's what adding value is all about.

RD: How can someone over forty get and keep a good job?

BS: That isn't rocket science. Let's say Pete Jones lost his job at a corporation in downtown Manhattan. Well, Jones has to look himself in the mirror and figure out what he has to offer to someone who has a job opening. He can't feel sorry for himself and decide that he's washed up. The key is to determine where Jones has made a contribution in the past and where he can make one in the future. When he figures that out, then he's ready to tell an employer what he can do. Incidentally, it's no shame to need a job. At some point in our careers, all of us have needed a job. The shame comes with self-pity.

Also, I'd advise Jones to make it a full-time job to look for a job. He has to tell everyone he meets how he can do jobs with no extra training, without close supervision, without needing to be motivated every two minutes. Jobs frequently come through the person we're sitting next to on the commuter train or in the barber shop.

Since the stock-market crash of 1987, about once a week someone over forty comes into my office and says, "Bob, I'm fifty-two and I need a job. How am I ever going to get one?" I tell him not to tell me his troubles, but rather to tell me how he's going to do the job better than anyone else. From my experience, if someone over forty can't get a good job it's because they're doing it to themselves. When I take the train into work, I see a lot of gray hair. Those people are going to good jobs—otherwise they couldn't afford the $200-plus-per-month train ticket.

RD: All the business experts say that we have to continue to learn. It's almost become a cliché. Do you think they're overstating the need to pick up new concepts and skills? After all, Bob, you don't have a word processor in your office.

BS: I don't need to do my own word processing as long as I am aware of the capabilities of the machine. I have my assistant do it. Valuable time spent learning is the critical issue here. I've decided that one of the most important management jobs I have is to manage how I use my time. I've also learned what the Internet has to offer, and I can ask any of our staff associates to research a project for me. Sure, there may be times when I should be doing my own word processing, on-line searches, and e-mail, but that time isn't now.

There's a prejudice in some offices that you can't teach an old dog new tricks. Well, those of us who want to keep our jobs will take the initiative to learn new things that will help us add value. For example, I add value in this office because of my ability to work well with the interns and young associates. I made it my job to understand them. I would study résumés from young people and find out what they wanted. I would also take the time to talk with young people to get a feel for what was important to them. Another way I add value is through learning how to deal with global clients. When I had an account based in Mexico, I got up to speed on all the factors that were affecting business in Mexico.

RD: One of the most important tools in a career is the ability to work the grapevine. Is it hard for someone your age to get access?

BS: Accessing the grapevine is important at any age. I make it a point to talk, listen, and ask plenty of questions. That's how I get the information I need. Because I've been around a while I sense what's happening, and if I ask the right questions I can get the information I want quickly. Smart bosses encourage all workers to get into the grapevine. It contains the company's crown jewels.

* * *

THE WHOLE ENCHILADA

Stone has survived because he recognizes that his image as a consummate professional must be constantly maintained and reinforced. If you want to be taken seriously as a productive employee—no matter what your age—you have to do everything right. Not just some things. For example, Stone acts appropriately hungry. Financially he may be comfortable, but the name of the game is to push for more of the goodies. Stone frequently comes into my office and asks what he has to do to get a bigger bonus—and many years he does get a bigger bonus than he did the year before.

INFLUENCE

How people see us, no matter what our age, doesn't require cosmetic surgery. Harrison Ford is still a leading heartthrob, and he's no spring chicken. Disney CEO Michael Eisner is in his fifties and has had bypass surgery. Still, he fits in great with the youthful ambience of Disney. In the media, we read about all the new ideas Eisner is implementing and the acquisitions he's making. His image is that of the "with it" executive. (Incidentally, when he had his heart surgery he kept working from his bed; he didn't withdraw into his illness.)

APPROACHING AGING STRATEGICALLY

How we present ourselves to the world as we age requires careful planning, but most of that is common sense. A fifty-year-old woman in Pittsburgh accepted a job that required an hour's commute over back roads. People at work would ask about the commute but she never bit—she never complained. Had she complained, any enemies she had in the firm would have had additional ammunition—like the commute was tiring her out.

As we age, we have to take frequent inventory of what we're losing and what we're gaining. We may be losing our speed. We can compensate for that by working more at home or putting in longer hours at the office. We also can get started on deadline assignments as soon as possible. We may be losing our razor-sharp memory, which means we may have to take more notes. We may be losing our endurance, which means maybe we should take breaks during the workday and stay longer in the evening. A colleague of mine reads an article in a magazine every few hours. That refreshes him and he can return to his work alert.

On the plus side, we have accumulated wisdom about fads in the business, and we can share it in a low-key manner. We might point out the mediocre track records that fads have had at the company. Or we may have developed patience—that may make us an ideal team member to develop new and complex products. We have to let the powers that be know that we have that trait. If we have become a good teacher, we can mentor the young people in the department. Companies have been looking for ways to institute mentoring programs.

When it comes to our assets, we have to do our own public relations. We have to let people know what we can offer.

WHAT YANKELOVICH SAYS

In many ways, the social research firm Yankelovich Partners was ahead of its time. Long before the aging workforce became an issue, the firm hired older workers to help out, even though Yankelovich is a "young person's" company. Also, in the late 1970s, Yankelovich flagged corporate America that workers' values were changing—that helped change many human resources policies.

Arthur White, currently vice chairman, is a founder of the firm. He loves exploring all the new questions that come up in his work. You might say that this mental activity helps keep him vigorous. He describes the Yankelovich atmosphere as a lot like college: The employees work on many diverse, challenging problems; they are supposed to do breakthrough thinking; and emphasis is on excellence.

* * *

INTERVIEW WITH ARTHUR WHITE

RD: You say the firm is a "young" company. Could you explain that?

AW: Our approach to questions is "young." We attract young people from college and graduate school to work here; it's an environment they slide into easily. But we have all parts of the life cycle represented. People tend to stay here, so you'll see many older workers.

In addition, we have a senior council. My dad was its first member. He was sixty-five and had just retired. When I was describing a project we planned for IBM, he said that he could help us with it. The senior council now has many retired executives who interview for our research. In their interviewing they demonstrate maturity, knowledge of business, and insights into human nature, which works out for both sides. We have good interviewers, and because they're part-time, they can take a few weeks off whenever they want to do something else.

RD: Do you think older employees are stereotyped in the workplace?

AW: There is tension in the workplace when someone hits sixty. You don't see that so much around those in their forties and fifties, but those in their sixties and in good health want to keep working. Then there is resentment on the part of younger people that older employees are taking up a slot that could open up for them. You're seeing a lot of this in education—teachers who have tenure and won't retire. That keeps other candidates from working as teachers. Those who want those jobs find reasons to not think well of the older incumbents.

RD: Are there positive stereotypes of older workers?

AW: Yes, many older workers have a work ethic that includes loyalty to the company. They thought they were getting a good deal—including benefits—and they went the extra mile for employers. But, as you know, this belief system isn't current today. In the 1960s, some people started to question what workers owed employers. Loyalty has become controversial.

RD: Are all workers over sixty treated the same?

AW: There are differences, which I found among several companies. Today, young people treat me with respect, but if I weren't vital there would be a prejudice about my age. I think that the age issue has confused many people. I get many calls from professionals in their fifties who may have been forced out. Maybe they don't like what they're doing. Maybe they sense the end is near. I advise them to put together some combination of work that will bring in revenues—if they need the money—and nonprofit work, which will allow them to make a contribution to society. In our later years we can really make a difference. Professionals in their fifties and sixties and beyond are finding that volunteer work is very satisfying.

Let me say that professionals in their fifties and sixties are essentially in shock. Their game plan has been upset by downsizing and whatnot, so they're looking to the previous generation—my generation—for guidance.

RD: How should professionals counteract negative stereotypes?

AW: I have several suggestions. One is to take care of your health. If you wake up in the morning and feel that you don't have the energy to do anything, you're going to be inert. But if your health is good you're ahead of the game. Next, make yourself aware of opportunities. There are a lot of people out there with needs—we have to figure out how to meet them. There are many, many ways to make a significant contribution—in local communities, at the state level, even at the national level. Third, realize that you don't need a full-time job to feel whole. There is a lot of work to get done that isn't packaged as a full-time job. If you feel good about yourself and your work, no one can put you down.

RD: Do you think that Ted Turner and Warren Buffett are role models of older, successful Americans?

AW: Not really. They made a lot of money. That's how people see them. Their age isn't important.

RD: What should the powers that be do for the aging worker?

AW: What's important is to prevent aging workers from feeling like they're dated. They are still needed in our society. There should be more career planning and training. We should be able to anticipate when a person might start losing his or her bearings in a profession, and we should have a solution for that. Our educational system has to be revamped to help in this issue of a lifetime of work.

* * *

Now You Know...

- We all age, but we're only seen as "old" if we act "old."
- Our lifestyles help prevent us from becoming "old," so we have to keep trying new things.
- Our image as productive professionals has to be integrated.
- We can't fall asleep at the wheel.
- Work does not have to mean full-time, paid employment to make us whole.

2

BOSSES

There's magic in the superior-subordinate relationship when we figure out what we can do to make the superior look good. This is true at any age.

—Cathleen Black, president of Hearst Magazines

What Do I Do?

- Our company is having problems. Should I put my energy into looking for another job or help the bosses fix the problems?
- The boss likes young MBAs. I'm not young, and I don't have an MBA.
- My new boss is younger than I am.
- I feel like I'm playing defense. Every day I feel that I have to show my boss that I still have the right stuff.
- I look in the mirror and see a fifty-four-year-old woman. The only way I'll be able to keep a job is to be indispensable to the boss.

BOSSES, BOSSES, BOSSES—PLENTY OF THEM

Few of us probably thought that we would get to this age and *still* have so many bosses. In fact, there are more bosses now than when I started out in business.

Today, in addition to the boss, there are shareholders to worry about. Team leaders to please. Colleagues and subordinates who evaluate us in comprehensive performance reviews. Customers whose loyalty we can no longer assume. Clients who demand something new and different all the time. In addition, there's that next person whom we want to be our boss and whom we have to impress now. There are also those critical ten or twenty people in our network whom we have to keep happy. Plus, a number of our former bosses still expect us to treat them like bosses.

Today, to hold on to our jobs or run our own businesses, we have to serve many masters. Gone are the days when we just had to worry about pleasing one boss.

AND OUR AGE

In addition to having all these masters to serve, there is also the reality of our chronological age. We're over forty.

This is the first time we've been forty, or fifty, or sixty—or seventy. And for many of us it's a puzzle how to conduct ourselves in professional life "at our age." We never *were* this age before. Should our persona be self-assured or enthusiastic? Should we confess our ignorance as we did in our youth? Should we figure that we've paid our dues and not go the extra mile? Or should we look for opportunities to make a contribution?

YOUNGER BOSSES

Many of our bosses and clients are now younger than we are. Should we defer to the younger boss or treat him or her like a partner? In her autobiography *Personal History*, the *Washington Post*'s Katharine Graham said she was delighted when her subordinate, Ben Bradlee, treated her as a partner. But some other bosses, no matter what their age, want it to be clear who's the boss.

In addition, when we're working with clients who are younger than we are, should we be maternal or paternal, or should we be all business? How can we not be awkward when our young client is an investment banker making ten times what we are? Are we prepared to meet a young client at a gym and work out next to her?

OUR HISTORY

How much "history" should we introduce when trying to solve problems at the office? What knowledge from the past is helpful to the organization? Does anyone care how Pepsi-Cola marketed soft drinks in 1970? When the Iacocca team came in to turn Chrysler around, they didn't want to hear a thing about the past. There's a fine line between introducing historical data that gives perspective and coming across as someone stuck in the past.

STEREOTYPES

Then there are all those stereotypes about what "older" workers are like. When the boss sees a sixty-year-old accountant, does she see an asset or someone to be pushed out? In this chapter, we'll look at these issues and discover strategies for handling them.

WHAT WE'RE UP AGAINST

The facts can be pretty brutal about what people in organizations, including bosses, think of older workers. In *The Fountain of Age*, Betty Friedan points out that there are negative perceptions about all older people.[1] To be older is to be placed in a perceptual ghetto. Our culture is hardwired to see older workers as something to be tolerated. When we see an older cashier at the drug store, we expect the transaction to take longer than if the worker were younger.

The growing field of gerontology—or the study of aging—isn't helping matters. Robert Atchley, Ph.D., who directs the Scripps Gerontology Center and is a professor of gerontology at Miami University of Ohio, is among those who are convinced that research about aging emphasizes the negative.[2] Therefore, the burden of proof is on us to demonstrate that we aren't the kinds of professionals portrayed by the negative stereotypes of older workers. We can't expect the boss to be "enlightened" and somehow know that we are on the ball despite our chronological age.

A recent career column in the *Wall Street Journal* confirms what we all know, namely, that superiors hesitate to offer constructive criticism to older employees. Doing so is stressful and the superiors tend to think, why do it if the older employee just has a short time to stay with the company?[3] But it's our responsibility to show our superiors that we are in it for the long term and that we are interested in constructive criticism.

We have few precedents for what we are doing. Never before in history have so many professionals over forty tried to make a living. In the *AARP Bulletin*, Robert Lewis points out that the national trend toward early retirement bottomed out in 1985. A growing number of the seventy-six million aging baby boomers indicate that they want to work as long as possible.[4] According to the *Wall Street Journal*, about 80 percent of baby boomers plan to work even after they officially retire.[5]

THE STRATEGIC APPROACH

For twenty or thirty years we have been approaching problems in our professional lives strategically. Now we've got to apply those same skills to managing the boss. For an older worker, managing the boss is as much a matter of strategic planning as increasing the market share of widgets or diversifying a product line. Our tools include:

- **Talking with other bosses and other employees about work issues in general — and listening.** Right now the workplace is one big learning laboratory in which we're all finding out how to be older *and* employable. This chapter includes an interview I had with a boss who's known to be an effective leader and an interview with a worker who has an outstanding track record for keeping bosses happy. They give insights about what's going on, but these are just the tip of the iceberg. We all need to do our own digging for information and perspective. A lot of the networking now going on is focused on finding out how older workers can thrive in the new economy.

  In addition to talking and listening, we have to become alert observers: We can take the role of anthropologists observing a strange tribe. Who over forty is getting the axe in that tribe? Who isn't? I know men and women over forty who have survived every reorganization. Who's getting promoted? Who gets invited to the boss's cabin cruiser?

- **Analyzing what the boss wants.** Here we better be right. There's no one way we should act in the workplace. What we do depends on what the boss wants us to do. Evaluation of performance is all relative, and bosses judge us by their needs and how we're meeting them—not by some abstract notion of "good" performance.

There's a dirty secret about the workplace that no one wants to tell: not every task can get done—or at least not done well. By planning strategically we can concentrate on the tasks that will get us recognition in the boss's eyes.

- **Figuring out how to deliver what the boss wants.** Those older workers who survive regime after regime are Zeligs. They are infinitely adaptable. They know how to reconfigure themselves into efficient machines who give bosses what they want. At a food company, there was a vice president of planning who managed to serve a number of presidents well. He's still there. At the "new" IBM, those who couldn't adjust to Lou Gerstner's leadership priorities were forced to go elsewhere.

- **Keep monitoring what makes the boss happy costs you spiritually, emotionally, and physically.** There's a qualitative difference between selling our soul and making mature compromises. Some of us are more than willing to work long hours. That's a necessary compromise in the global marketplace, but none of us should be willing to endure degrading conditions. There are bosses we shouldn't be working for.

The rest of this chapter will give you tips on developing a strategy for dealing with the boss.

STRATEGY ONE: TALKING, LISTENING, AND WATCHING

A lot of general information and wisdom we need to deal with our individual bosses is out there, only it's not in books—at least not yet. The new rules about being an older worker are just being formed. In five years, the Harvard Business School will probably have a course on how older workers manage to keep their bosses happy, but for now we've got to wing it.

We get the skinny on how we can dazzle our bosses by talking and listening. As with anything new, everyone is talking about what's going on in their own business and with older workers. They're talking about how worker X, who's seventy, has survived every reorganization, and about worker Y, who's fifty and just started an internal mentoring program for employees of all ages—and his boss *loves* it.

We can listen to bosses reveal what they like about their older employees. If we hear the word *even* ten times in terms of older workers' temperaments, we can probably conclude that many bosses like even-tempered staff. That's certainly a clue to stop being a rebel or a hothead. In addition, we can watch successful older employees. Do all of them go the extra mile? Stay cool in a crisis? Protect the boss in meetings?

CATHLEEN BLACK, PRESIDENT OF HEARST MAGAZINES

One person I've been talking with, listening to, and watching for her style of interaction is Cathleen Black. She is the first woman to ever be named president of Hearst Magazines, a division of the Hearst Corporation. She's been appearing on all kinds of lists of powerful women, but her performance should be evaluated gender free. Black is one of the contemporary business world greats who is putting a unique imprint on communications.

At Hearst, Black oversees the financial performance and development of some of the magazine industry's best-known titles, including *Esquire, Harper's Bazaar, Popular Mechanics, Redbook, Good Housekeeping,* and *Town and Country*. In addition, she has extended the brand names of Hearst's titles beyond magazines to more than three thousand products, and she has overseen the group's expansion into the new world of electronic media.

* * *

INTERVIEW WITH CATHLEEN BLACK

RD: You're not comfortable with the term *boss*, are you?

CB: It's not so much a question of whether I'm comfortable with the term as it is a question of how it defines professional interaction in the workplace. It's a fact that almost everyone reports to someone— regardless of where you stand within a company. But I don't like the rigid hierarchy that the word *boss* implies. It's not my way of managing people.

RD: In your experience, what makes for a successful workplace relationship?

CB: The best relationships occur when the manager is crystal clear about expectations and there is no ambiguity about an individual's role. So, in reality, communication is key to a successful professional relationship—or any relationship, for that matter.

RD: How do we go about creating a strong and productive relationship between a superior and ourselves?

CB: It begins with the manager. It is important that she make herself accessible to her people. And she needs to be direct. If your staff can't get to you—or understand what you expect of them—it won't be smooth sailing, to say the least.

When it comes to creating a strong and productive relationship with your manager, make sure you understand what is expected of you. The manager should define the expectations, but it's your job to make sure you make sense of it. Also, if your manager isn't accessible and direct, you may have to read between the lines a little. Take a look around and see how others deal with him or her and take your cue from them.

RD: At lunch or on personal phone calls, I hear a lot of muttering about dealing with a younger boss. Can you suggest strategies for dealing with this situation?

CB: Dealing with that situation may require adjustment on both sides. For the younger boss, it means a certain degree of empathy and tact. For the older subordinate, he or she should keep in mind that the boss probably wants new approaches to the job—and shouldn't be second-guessed because of his or her youth. The younger boss surely doesn't want to hear "We've done it that way and it doesn't work." In other words, fewer examples of past experience are better when dealing with a younger boss or older subordinate.

RD: When bosses have subordinates, do they say in their heads, "Oh, that worker is old, or that worker acts old"?

CB: I wouldn't put it that way, but I will say that people need to adjust to an ever-changing work environment. It's essential that people keep their clothing, language, and references current. You don't want to be perceived as being out of sync with the times.

RD: What have you learned dealing with older employees?

CB: A lot. I particularly remember a salesman named Jack. We all learned from him. I was in my mid-thirties and Jack applied for a job within my group. He was in his mid-fifties, and I didn't think that he was a good fit for our organization. He got a job elsewhere, but later we bought the company that he worked for, so he joined us. Within six months, he became the number-one person on the sales staff, but more than that, he shared his expertise with the group and made time to train rookie salespeople in the fine art of client relationships. He thought "young" and was always coming up with new ideas. He completely won my respect and that of everyone on the team.

RD: From Jack, I guess you've learned that aging is an individual process. Some can be thirty and "old" while others can be fifty and professionally effective.

CB: Right, Bob. Jack worked with us for about ten years. He's in his mid-seventies now and we still stay in touch. You can make generalizations. It depends on the individual.

* * *

Black has pointed out that it's up to older workers to adjust to new realities—and to keep adjusting. It's unlikely that the workplace is going to change to accommodate us.

Another key point Black made is that aging is idiosyncratic. There are the Robert Byrds of the Senate who remain energetic and feisty and the Richard Nixons who seem to be born "old."

RICHARD KOSMICKI

In our office, Richard Kosmicki is the prince of media relations. He knows how to get a story placed anywhere in print, on the electronic media, and in cyberspace. But Kosmicki's talents go beyond his job description. He helps make me, his boss, look good. I see Kosmicki as an asset and a "value added," not an "older worker." Kosmicki has been in the work force for some forty-eight years, most of them serving Fortune 100 clients. Because he knows how to manage the boss, Kosmicki will be working as long as he chooses—and making top dollar.

* * *

INTERVIEW WITH RICHARD KOSMICKI

RD: Over the years you've had a number of high-profile bosses, such as the Tisch brothers at Loew's and Joe Flavin at Singer. You've made them look good. At our firm, you're one of my most valuable players. What are you doing right?

RK: Even back in the days when I was a proofreader on a newspaper in upstate New York, I "got it" that my success depended on the success of my boss. If he or she looked good, I looked good. If the boss failed, I failed—both in terms of the job and how I saw myself.

To put that in more concrete terms, if I want the boss to be successful, I'll learn all about the business. I'll understand how the firm works and what its image is. I'll understand what kind of clients the boss is trying to attract. If you want to help the boss make home runs, you can't just come in and do your job. You have to dig around and envision the big picture. If I grasp the big picture, then I can serve as sort of an internal "consultant" to the boss and help with decision-making.

RD: We all make mistakes. How do you handle mistakes with a boss?

RK: I've made my share of mistakes during my thirty years in public relations. They were of two kinds. One is the interactional mistake—either I didn't read the boss's mood right and the boss got annoyed or distracted, or I made a suggestion at the wrong time. The second kind of mistake is task-oriented. I didn't get enough publicity for a client or I didn't properly prepare the client for a negative article. For both kinds of mistakes, I have the same modus operandi. I admit that I'm wrong—to myself and to all parties involved. I think that's called "owning" your part of the problem. Next, I pull out all stops to fix the situation, and I keep at it until the situation is 100 percent fixed. That might take months.

RD: You've been in the game a long time. Have you changed on how your work with your superiors over time?

RK: Generally, no. I keep the same mind-set, the same discipline. In a recent issue of *Forbes*, management consultant Peter Drucker notes that the boss is the boss is the boss. Sure there are flattened hierarchies, but there will always be someone with the final authority in the department or organization. My idea of the "boss" is basically the same I had as a young man.

What has changed is my ability to be completely open with the boss. Now that I'm older, there's less to risk. My children are grown and I have savings, so I have less to lose. As a result of being more open, I am more valuable to the boss. Also, when I was younger, I assumed that the boss knew more than I did. Now I realize that I know some things that the boss doesn't know or doesn't care to know.

RD: I haven't been able to define it. But there's something unique that makes our relationship work. Why do you think we can be so effective as a team?

RK: The chemistry is right—but we're talented in different ways. So, when we're trying to solve a problem, we need each other. We're both smart enough to recognize that. Also, our values are the same—sort of old-world. We both believe in integrity and hard work. You also make yourself accessible. Days don't go by that I can't get in to see you. I guess what I'm saying is that certain prerequisites must exist before people can form a strong team. The chemistry has to be there, and we can't be redundant in our talents and skills. Also, the belief systems have to be similar, and you have to be available to me, no matter how busy we get.

RD: Have you ever had a boss who wasn't a good fit for you?

RK: Yes. It really affected my productivity. The chemistry was wrong. That particular boss was a bully with mediocre ability, which led me to live in fear and uncertainty—I didn't speak up when I should have. It got to the point where I became ineffecient because much of my energy was going into watching or monitoring myself. From that experience, I've learned not to accept a job where the chemistry between myself and the boss is off.

RD: As you know, I'm younger than you in years. Does that present any special challenges to you?

RK: Age, per se, is not an issue, at least not with me. With the boss, the issue is respect. Do I respect the boss's character? Do I respect the boss's accomplishments? If I do, then we're going to work together very well.

RD: In addition to being a subordinate to me, you're a boss to at least four people. How do you communicate to them what you expect?

RK: I just spell out what I want, face-to-face, whenever the need arises. "In-your-face" communication reduces ambiguity and miscommunications. Someone sees my face, my eyes, and hears my voice.

They see my body language. So they usually understand what they have to do.

RD: Suppose you were considering changing jobs. How would you find out if Joe Smith at General Widget is the right kind of boss for you?

RK: I'd make it my business to talk to people there *before* I became a serious candidate for the job. I'd take due diligence seriously. Through networking, you can always get the name of someone who works there. You can call that person and don't have to be direct. You can read between the lines regarding what they say about Joe Smith and the corporate culture. Ask if there is anyone else you can talk to—maybe someone who left the organization. What about talking with suppliers? Externally, you can speak with reporters about what's going on in the organization. They have probably dealt with the boss. You can check databases and the Internet to see if there is any information about the boss or the corporate culture. This kind of homework is a must-do before anyone takes a new job.

* * *

Probably the most significant insight Richard Kosmicki has about the boss-subordinate relationship is that subordinates have to go beyond the tasks of their immediate job. If they are going to help bosses shine, they have to understand the boss's goals on a macro level.

STRATEGY TWO: ANALYZING WHAT THE BOSS WANTS

What the boss wants may have nothing to do with the department or company. The boss might want a reputation outside the company. That means we have to help her develop a high profile in her industry, in business, or nonprofits. Perhaps we can make an impression on her by writing provocative speeches for her or introducing her to movers and shakers.

It takes work to piece together what's really important to the boss. At first, on the surface, all we might see is a very ambitious person who obviously wants to climb the ladder in the company. But most bosses also have a more private agenda. Typically, they have missions they want to accomplish. At the former Gulf Oil, Bill Moffett, the head of public affairs during the energy shortage, wanted to position the company and its top executives as issue leaders in energy. If you understood that and helped make it happen, you would probably do well with Moffett. If you did your job in a vacuum and didn't use it to help move the ball on Moffett's agenda, you weren't going to be one of his most valuable players.

How do we ferret out what bosses want? It's imperative that we network and gather information about the boss from past associates, current associates, and outsiders. When the late Dan Hirshfield came to Chrysler in the early 1980s, some of his subordinates checked with headhunters and Hirshfield's former associates at his last job at Union Carbide to find out what mattered to him.

Sometimes it's possible to ask the boss about his goals directly. There is a growing number of executives who are candid about what they really want. When Lee Iacocca was being pressured to retire during the succession crisis at Chrysler, a few executives let it be known that they wanted to be the next CEO. At Honeywell, Chief Financial Officer Chris Steffen made it clear that he wanted to be the next CEO.

We can analyze the boss's communications, everything from speeches to e-mail. If you read the executives' speeches at IBM during the 1980s, you'd "get it" fast that the bosses wanted to maintain the status quo. If you read Nabisco CEO John Greenius's speeches during the 1980s, you knew he wanted to increase growth in the business.

In addition, we can be alert to whom the boss promotes, socializes with, and hires. Look for patterns. What defeats have had the most impact on the boss? If the boss considers an event a significant defeat, then we have clues about that person's agenda. When the investor relations function at Gulf was moved from public affairs to an autonomous place in the organization, Bill Moffett seemed to be upset. That told the organization that he felt that control over how shareholders perceived Gulf was an essential part of his responsibilities.

STRATEGY THREE: DELIVERING RESULTS
IN THE RIGHT PACKAGING

Not all results are equal. Getting results for the boss won't get us much unless we deliver them in a way that the boss likes. Employee A writes an innovative speech for the boss, but there's no pat on the back for him. That's because the speech arrived on his boss's desk after the deadline. There were typos in it, and references to movies the executive never saw. As a result, the executive has a bad feeling about the experience, even though the speech was good. Employee A should have asked around about how the executive liked to work. Employee B brought in the results of an important project and told the boss, in detail, all the obstacles she had encountered. The boss wasn't interested in hearing about how the project got done, and in the boss's eyes, employee B's stock went down.

THE PACKAGING

How we deliver results shapes how a project is perceived. Here are some common errors in packaging:

- **Too much time and interactional stress.** Most bosses want to assume that quality results will be delivered on time and in the required format. That's what delegation is all about. They also don't want any surprises, so the executive should be kept informed of any significant developments. At Singer, a writer was canned for asking too many questions and spending too much time discussing strategies. It might not be legal to do that, but it's done all the time. Bosses won't tolerate employees who rob them of their time or cause them angst.

- **Creating enemies.** Fine results could be perceived negatively if a worker alienated too many people in the process. The typical culprit here is the go-getter who obtained results at others' expense. Go-getters might have bruised other folks' egos, been piggy about using resources, made promises that weren't kept, and misrepresented information. Those go-getters are usually quickly benched or fired. Bosses want employees who know how to conduct themselves in an organization. It's imperative to understand the corporate culture and how things get done in that culture.

- **Stealing the show.** Bosses get to be bosses because they understand the importance of image. When it comes to recognition, they usually want to be numero uno. During the Iacocca period at Chrysler, a public relations person asked a finance executive if he also wanted an article done on him. The executive wisely declined. He was experienced enough in organizational dynamics to realize that Iacocca wouldn't want to share the spotlight.

Bosses are the ones who define how much recognition will be given to others. In academia, their name usually goes first on a research article. In productive development, the boss's name goes down in history as the point person. At Chrysler, Hal Sperlich became known as the "father" of the minivan. Some of this can be negotiated, but basically the leader will take most of the credit—and most leaders will help the careers of those who helped them. Those of us who get too close to the spotlight will be ousted.

- **Being a jerk.** There are infinite ways that any of us can alienate the boss by being what is commonly known as a jerk, even though our work is splendid. In this case, wit or humor can be especially dangerous. At Chrysler, a group of professionals had a long-standing joke about an executive who used football analogies. The executive got wind of it and punished the culprits. The relationship wasn't the same after that. One employee explicitly told a superior that she didn't like to be contacted at home. She lost power. A naive worker, assuming that performance evaluations were very important, amended his. The boss was ticked off.

    Jerks get under the boss's skin and frequently cause embarrassment. At Gulf, Moffett made pets of those who were sophisticated enough not to do what jerks do.

* * *

STRATEGY FOUR: EVALUATING THE COST OF COMPROMISES

Every year, *Fortune* magazine lists the toughest bosses in America. I worked for several of them, and every one of those experiences helped my career. If they hadn't, I wouldn't have stayed very long in any of those jobs. What to endure and for what payoff is an individual choice. The responsibility to do the math is ours—not the boss's.

A member of the U.S. Senate was crude. One of the women who

worked for him couldn't take it and found another job. Another woman blew it off and used the job as a way of getting connected around Washington, D.C. Who was right? Both. Unlike the 1950s, when success meant a job, a car, a house in the suburbs, and a family, there are many definitions of success today. The *Wall Street Journal* reports that Roanoke College in Salem, Virginia, offers a course exploring different views of success.[6]

Pepsi executive Brenda Barnes is an example of the new approaches that define *success*. Barnes decided that her job was taking too much time from her family life. So she left the job to make her family life more successful. Some say Barnes was shortsighted, but what really matters is what Barnes says to herself. Like her, we have choices today.

To choose wisely, we have to be all grown up. We have to understand the trade-offs in the work world, and we have to understand ourselves. Then we have to decide what road we're going to travel.

Young people may be better at this than we are. I hear many people in their twenties say that they'll go to a sweatshop-type place for two years, then leave and leverage that credential. They accept that they will have virtually no personal life for those two years. To them it's worth it. We have to treat our careers in the same analytic fashion. And we must be willing to leave jobs that cost us too much.

Now You Know...

- Many bosses do have a negative perception of older workers, and it's our responsibility to change that perception.
- The key to success with bosses is to make them look good.
- We've got to find out on our own how older workers can survive and thrive in the new workplace. We do this by talking, listening, and watching; by analyzing what the boss really wants; by delivering results in the right packages; and by examining what working with a particular boss is costing us.
- *Success* now has many different definitions.

3

FREE AGENTS CAN FINISH FIRST

*As more and more people declare free agency, a genuine market—
with brokers, exchanges, and an evolving set of rules—is emerging
for their talent.*

—Daniel Pink, "The Talent Market"

HAVE TALENT—CAN HOP AROUND

The majority of those working at our firm are over fifty—and many
of them are free agents. They've been talking about free agents in
sports for years, but the term *free agent* is new in offices and is often
interchangeable with consultant. A free agent is a professional who
recognizes his or her own talent and is willing and able to negotiate a
fair or even premium fee for his or her work—usually for a specific
assignment or group of assignments. Leigh Steinberg, one of the most
powerful agents in sports, now gives advice on how to negotiate deals
to free agents in areas other than sports.[1] Professional organizations
are also helping free agents get the right compensation. Free agents
who know what they're doing can earn six figures.

HOW FREE AGENTS OPERATE

In Manhattan, there are at least three executive search firms that
handle free agents in communications. Soon there will be more.
These firms place professionals in appropriate assignments for a day,
week, or sometimes a year or more. Free agents go to offices to do

39

their assignments, work from home, stay on the road, and keep in touch through e-mail. Often, when free agents acquire new skills and experience they redo their résumé, put together a new pitch, and up their rates.

There are now so many free agents, says the *New York Times*, that no one, including the government, knows how many of them there are.[2]

WHAT'S IN IT FOR YOU?

Being a free agent isn't for everybody. Some people require the unchanging, structured environment of a formal office to work effectively. Many start scouting around for full-time jobs after a few years out there on their own. The biggest reason for returning to the fold is the sense of belonging, the regular checks, and the benefits. Additionally, part of being a free agent is constantly being on the prowl for new assignments. Many free agents quickly tire of the perpetual marketing. However, some of these free agents who return to traditional jobs can't readjust to the rules of the workplace and go out on their own again. Freelance writer Mary Jane Genova was a free agent for about seven years. Then she grew weary of the constant marketing and took a full-time job with an insurance company in Hartford. She hated getting up in the morning with an alarm clock to be somewhere at a certain time; putting on a suit and nylons; having a boss observe her all day; attending myriad meetings; and putting in face time after 5:00 P.M. "I got spoiled as a free agent," she reports. "If you're talented you can usually call the shots on the terms and conditions of your assignments. No one bothers you. The trade-off is that you have to become an efficient marketing machine."

For those with the right temperament, being a free agent offers the best of the work-world options. Here are some of the major advantages:

- Free agents can "hire" and "fire" their clients. If they have a client who is difficult or doesn't pay well, they can phase that client out. Being able to choose with whom you will work eliminates a lot of misery.

- Free agents have more control over the security of their work situation. If you're a corporate worker, your job is at the mercy of management. In hard times, free agents can market more or in different ways. They can adjust pricing. They can learn a new skill and offer it in the marketplace.

- Free agents have time flexibility—it's no longer a big deal to schedule a dental appointment.
- Being a free agent often eliminates the need to excel in office politics. Although free agents usually have to network for their assignments, they don't have to be highly skilled in "playing the game." Also, if a free agent does make a political mistake, she won't feel the brunt of it as an employee would because she is her own boss. She may lose a client, but not her job.
- There is usually no age discrimination in being a free agent. The vice president of public affairs who might use a sixty-year-old with the right skills for a certain assignment might not hire that person for a full-time job.
- It's possible to build up a real retirement nest egg by socking away a percentage of earnings into Keoghs, and for free agents, everything put into a retirement plan is deducted from earnings before the income is taxed. This is especially attractive to older professionals who left corporate life with no pensions.
- Not only is it possible to do creative work, a fresh perspective is usually demanded of freelancers. Reports Mary Jane Genova, "In corporate life, I remember writing up a media presentation with an analogy to *Star Wars*. The client, an engineer, hit the roof. In freelancing I have to pitch new ideas *even before* I get an assignment. Before a client hires me they want to make sure that I'm thinking out-of-the-box."
- Without the pressures of a full-time job, it's possible to get a life. Many free agents discover how satisfying volunteer work is. Free agents can spend time with grandchildren. One free agent got a degree in creative writing on the side.
- More and more employment firms such as MacTemps are springing up to screen, place, and handle the billing for free agents. Based in Dallas, MacTemps will even help free agents manage their careers.[3] This is ideal for free agents who don't want

to market themselves and worry about getting paid. To find out about these agencies, check the Yellow Pages under "Employment." Also, many standard search firms, such as the Cantor Concern in Manhattan, which handles communications, also provide interim placement.

THE DOWNSIDE

Being a free agent is not for everyone. One man in Pittsburgh who had been laid off refused a long-term assignment in a public relations agency because he was told that he would have to help bring in new business. He wanted no part of marketing. He wanted a traditional public relations job in which the work would come to him, he would get paychecks every two weeks, and he wouldn't have to wine and dine prospects. He was lucky. He did find an excellent public relations position with a small company. He had to move to Virginia, but he was willing to pay that price.

Some try to be a free agent and hate it. A manager at a telecommunications company who was making about $80,000 set up a little office in her home after she was forced out. That lasted about three months. She hated working at home. She hated being alone. She didn't have the confidence that she could ever match her former compensation through freelancing. Eventually she found a decent job at a small company.

There are a number of common pitfalls associated with being a free agent:

- It's an adjustment to go from being a full-time worker to being out there on your own. At parties you used to be able to say that you worked for such-and-such a corporation, and everyone seemed to know who you were and what you did. Now if you say that you're a consultant or a temporary worker, it isn't as clear who you are or what you do. Some might even assume that you're just unemployed. Until you're established as a free agent, you're apt to have a mini identity crisis.

- Whether you market yourself on your own or through an employment agency, you have to know how to position and package yourself to get work in the current marketplace. One woman went to a financial services firm unsure of what her skills were. The manager of communications bluntly told her that he wasn't going to do her marketing for her. It was her responsibility to create a match between what she could offer and what the marketplace needed.

As the market changes or your skills change, you will have to continue to reposition and repackage yourself. Being a free agent means being a work in progress.

- You have to provide everything for yourself that the job automatically gave you, ranging from social companionship to benefits. If you don't compensate for what you "lost," you're going to be unhappy as a free agent. One free agent got the social contact he needed by going to a support group in his city every day at noon.

  Benefits can be problematic. Getting the right ones takes work. For medical insurance, you might talk to an insurance broker who deals with a variety of insurance companies rather than represent just one company. By talking to an insurance broker in Connecticut, one free agent got just the right coverage for her situation. She signed up with a small carrier that offered $2,000 prescription coverage. Since she was on Prozac, which is very expensive, she got what she needed.

  For disability coverage, you might have to call a number of insurance companies to find out who offers disability and if you will qualify. One woman on a heart medication was rejected by most of the insurance carriers.

  As for Keoghs, you can talk with a financial planner or call a reputable company and ask for the names of a few. Interview possible planners until you feel safe with one. Some free agents also get themselves accountants and lawyers.

- Being the boss is tough. After years complaining about our boss, all of a sudden we become the person where the buck stops. If an assignment goes haywire, it's our baby. If a client quits, the loss directly hits our pocket. We might have to hire and fire.

  Here it could be helpful to read material on leadership. Way back in 1985, Warren Bennis and Burt Nanus wrote their landmark book *Leaders*, and it's still relevant today. For instance, the authors explain how leaders compensate for their own weaknesses.[4] Community colleges offer good seminars on leadership. Also, if you check the Internet you might find a course on leadership on-line. New magazines, such as *Business 2.0*, provide fresh insights on leadership in the digital age.

- There's a need to create one's own sense of purpose. The vision and mission of your former company are irrelevant now. One free agent's sense of purpose started out as just being able to survive for two years as a free agent. Then his mission evolved into becoming a brand name in his field. When he achieved that mission he began to do extensive pro bono work, which gave him great satisfaction.

  Not everyone can become mission-oriented. For years you might have gone to work just to pick up the check, and that was okay. But out there on your own you have to keep yourself rolling. If you're not good at designing goals for yourself, maybe this isn't for you.

- There's no guaranteed income. Every profession has its own pattern of demand. Business might be strong in three quarters and then slow down in fourth. During the off-season, free agents fall apart, both because new business isn't coming in and they become anxious about money. Many free agents have to change their mind-sets. They have to learn to consider themselves okay even when they're not working. They also have to learn to budget better.

- Not everyone respects your accomplishment. Relatives and friends might define *success* in terms of a traditional job with a traditional title.

THEY SAW IT COMING

Being a free agent might be new to some of us, but theorists about trends in the workplace have been predicting a gutting of the corporation's full-time staff and the creation of a just-in-time workforce. London Business School professor Charles Handy announced way back in 1989 that a new kind of organization was emerging. In *The Age of Unreason*, Handy said that the new organization would function like a shamrock. One leaf would be a small contingency of full-time workers. The other two leaves would be composed of just-in-time workers, ranging from freelancers to part-time employees.[5] Handy's prediction turned out to be right on the money. In the business media, he became the patron saint of the temporary work-force. I'm convinced that this trend will continue.

THE BUSINESS OF FREE AGENTS

In the *Fast Company* issue on talent, we can read about John Thompson. For thirty-five years he worked for the accounting firm KMG. Then the firm merged and Thompson was out of a job. That was 1987. By 1988, Thompson had put together an interim management firm called IMCOR. IMCOR grew from a modest enterprise to the premier interim management firm in the United States, with offices in Stamford, Chicago, Dallas, Los Angeles, Atlanta, and New York.[6]

JOHN THOMPSON

After I read about John Thompson, I decided that I wanted him to become part of this book. I wanted to find out how placing temporary professionals can become a business. When I spoke with Thompson, he told me that getting the business off the ground wasn't easy. When he met with executives in corporations about his plan, not too many were excited. But it turned out that Thompson read the market right. Today his average temporary worker has about two decades of experience, and they earn six figures. In 1997, Thompson's firm was purchased by Novell Services, a New York Stock Exchange company.

* * *

INTERVIEW WITH JOHN THOMPSON

RD: John, what was your transition like from being with a prestigious accounting firm to being out there on your own?

JT: When I retired from the accounting firm I looked at three things. I knew that I was good at running a service business. I was convinced that I could function as an entrepreneur. And I really enjoyed working with people. People were my passion.

That was one part of it. The second part was the marketplace. I felt that there was an undeserved market for people in their late forties and beyond who had a tremendous amount of talent but—through no fault of their own—had been terminated from their jobs. I knew that these people had a lot to offer, but they had no vehicle to get their story out and to present their credentials to the right people. Third, there was a need for these people on a short-term or assignment basis. The challenge was to link them together with the people who needed them. That's why I started IMCOR.

RD: In dealing with those seeking assignments, do you find that those over forty would prefer a permanent full-time job to working as a free agent?

JT: That depends very much on the individual. In my dealings with those over forty, I've found the core issue to be that they're concerned with being employable. They're less concerned with the form that employment takes, and the form is changing rapidly. Today, in addition to full-time permanent jobs, you have multiple jobs where someone works, say, two part-time jobs. You have people working full time in temporary assignments, people on contract or retainer, and people working from day to day.

RD: Do you find that people who are free agents feel less good about themselves?

JT: No. In fact they feel *better* about themselves than professionals with full-time jobs.

RD: Why is that?

JT: It's because contract workers are in control of their work. They are the boss. Many of them think of themselves as entrepreneurs. They have the freedom to do what they want to do. They can be more creative than people in conventional jobs.

RD: How does a free agent get in touch with IMCOR?

JT: It isn't hard. You can reach us on the Internet at IMCOR.com. We have a substantial presence there. We're also linked to many networking systems—Harvard Business School graduates, alumni of Stamford—you name it, we're probably linked. In addition, we're in conventional placement directories. You can probably find us in the Yellow Pages under "Executive Search."

RD: Do temporary assignments lead to full-time jobs?

JT: Usually the person who takes a temporary assignment is interested in long-term employability—not getting a job per se. But an assignment can lead to a job. If the person offered the job is interested, then it's a match, but anyone in that situation knows this does not mean getting a job for life. That job will eventually come to an end, and the person who was holding it will become a free agent again. What matters is not contract work versus full-time jobs but if the person has marketable skills and is employable.

RD: What do you look for in someone who wants to be placed by IMCOR?

JT: Up-to-date skills and know-how. If you're an accountant you have to be up-to-date. Also, the person should be a self-starter and understand how to work effectively with other people.

RD: What kind of growth do you see in the field of temporary employment?

JT: Exponential growth.

* * *

JUMPING IN

There are all kinds of ways to get started as a free agent.

EMPLOYMENT AGENCIES

The easiest way to start as a free agent is through employment agencies that use temporary help. Register with several agencies. Each one usually has different connections in the job market. One might have ties to Ford Motor Company and another might have ties to Honeywell.

If the agencies use scannable résumés it will be imperative for you to create a résumé that contains the keywords in your field. Your résumé will be automatically discarded if it doesn't have them. This is especially important if your skills involve technology.

In filling out application forms and talking with the intake counselor, make yourself as accessible as possible. Indicate that you are available in many different time slots, that you can work on-site, not just at home, that you're willing to travel, and so forth. One excellent candidate never got assignments because she was unwilling to work on-site.

Keep updating your credentials with the employment agencies. If you've learned PowerPoint, let them know. Also let them know about any recent accomplishments, such as saving the department 22 percent in paper costs.

HELP WANTED ADS

Another way to get into the loop is through help wanted ads, both in print and on the Internet. Here you have to pitch yourself and negotiate compensation on your own. But an agency isn't getting a piece of the action.

More and more ads are carrying the terms *part-time* or *temporary*. Here it's important that your cover letter and résumé exactly match what's needed. If you have to know Microsoft Word, you have to indicate that you do know it in your cover letter and résumé. Even with a temporary gig, it's imperative to fine-tune your standard cover letter and résumé to fit that particular situation.

Libraries carry out-of-town classified sections, and more and more free agents are looking at the want ads in areas to which they could commute. Also, companies may be willing to fly you to their facilities if you have the right set of skills.

DIRECT MAIL

A good direct mail campaign can also work. One woman used direct mail primarily the first year she was a free agent. She earned $90,000 that year—and that was 1988. Through direct mail she was able to tap into work opportunities out of her area. About 50 percent of her early business came from out of state.

In using direct mail, it's wise to keep the letter to one page and not include a résumé. A résumé usually gives the signal that you're looking for a full-time job. In the letter, state how you can be of use to the company. Discuss results you've obtained for other clients. Tell them that supporting credentials such as writing or product samples are available if they're required. On page 49, you will find a sample letter that got results.

Dear _____:

I just completed the graphics work on company X's award-winning annual report. I suggested to them that we use the millennium motif. It was a home run. I also handled the redesign of their employee communications vehicles.

Before that assignment I had helped with the graphics at Fortune 100 companies in everything from the Internet and brochures to point-of-purchase displays and new product design. My work won several awards, including the _____ and _____, and sales of products increased 32 percent in six months. I would like to assist your company with its graphics challenges.

If you would like to learn more about my services and fees, please contact my Web site at _____, or call me at _____. I'd love the opportunity to meet with you.

In a direct mail campaign the significant variables include:

- **The person the letter is addressed to.** Should you contact the head of the department or the CEO? You can get some help on this by contacting companies and finding out who is the best person to write to.
- **The return address on the envelope.** Some free agents use their own name and not the name of their company in the hopes that the mail won't be thrown out before it's opened. Companies receive thousands of letters from consultants. Most aren't opened.
- **What gimmicks, if any, lead the person to read the message.** Some free agents have good success sending postcards with provocative graphics instead of number-ten white envelopes.
- **What's in it for the reader to scan and respond to the message.** Right up-front in your letter, you have to tell the receiver what's in it for them if they do business with you.

ADVERTISING

Advertising is a wild card. A good ad can get enormous response but no actual business. The key ingredient here is to put the ad in the right publication or TV or radio spot. One ghostwriter put an ad in *New York Magazine* and got at least one hundred calls from people with little sophistication and less money.

Ask colleagues where they advertise and what kinds of results they get. Or, call other advertisers in the publication and ask how much actual business they get from their ads. Try a small ad initially and see what happens. Make sure you have all systems in place when you run an ad. For example, the Monday your ad appears in the *Wall Street Journal* don't plan to go out of town.

NETWORKING

Some free agents do their marketing by networking. They immediately join professional organizations and start doing volunteer work for the organizations, which quickly gets them known. Many assignments are made via word of mouth.

Although many free agents live from assignment to assignment, they have to take a long-term perspective. Networking is a long-term activity. You can't just go to one meeting of the IABC and expect a lot of business to start rolling in. Networking requires an investment of time, but the payoff can be tremendous.

GIVING A FINDER'S FEE

Smart free agents usually have a couple of scouts keeping an eye open for work for them. In return, these scouts get a percentage of the business they bring in. That percentage can range from 4 to 10 percent. This arrangement works well. Some people are just well connected. It's worth the finder's fee to plug into their sphere of influence.

PUBLISHING

Not only in the academic world is it "publish or perish." Publications also count when you are a free agent. One seven-hundred-word article in the *Speechwriters' Newsletter* got a free agent a new client. Just like that.

You can publish in trade publications, general newspapers, prestigious magazines, and books. Once these appear, you can send them with a personal note to clients and prospects. This strategy can work like a charm. One public relations person wrote an article on values in the late 1980s and sent it to prospects. It hit the right chord. New business came in.

QUALITY OF LIFE

For a growing number of professionals, at its core, being a free agent isn't just about getting enough business and piling up tax deductions. It's more and more about the quality of their lives. Kass Prezio of Baltimore, Maryland, worked for the government for twenty-two years. When she retired four years ago, she never considered getting another nine-to-five job. She was committed to doing the things she wanted to do when she wanted to do them. She wanted a balance between earning money to supplement her pension and enjoying her life.

* * *

INTERVIEW WITH KASS PREZIO, A FREE AGENT IN BALTIMORE

RD: Why did you retire from the government?

KP: I think there's a time in life for full-time jobs. My time was past. I had been working many years. I wanted to keep working in some form but not at a full-time job.

　　Also, I was tired of the image one has to maintain in full-time jobs. I felt that I had to dress a certain way. I had never worn slacks. I felt that I had not been able to say certain things. Also, I wanted to try new things. I've always been interested in antiques, and in doing volunteer work.

　　When the government offered me a package I was ready to retire. There was a small pension. Just as important, they provided health coverage. I knew that I would need that. I figured that I could make it without a full-time job and pay my mortgage with what I would receive from the government, and I was right.

RD: When did you start being a free agent?

KP: Before I left the government. I knew that I would continue working, and that I would be living about forty more years and I wanted those years to include working. Originally, I had intended to take a break, to take some time off after I left the government, but two months after I retired a project came to me. It had to do with the Internet and I didn't want to pass that opportunity up, so I jumped in.

RD: What else have you've done to earn money?

KP: Writing for organizations—speeches, brochures, articles. I've taught Spanish in a middle school. I sell antiques to consignment stores. I was a salesperson in a consignment store and that led to my decorating the windows and doing the books. I've been a trainer for the state of Maryland and have done investigations for equal employment opportunity cases associated with the federal government.

The nicest thing about all this is that I can do it more or less when I want to. I can go to the swimming pool during the day. I can shop for groceries at 10:00 A.M. instead of 6:00 P.M. when the stores are crowded. I can socialize with friends during the day, travel to see my family in the middle of the week, and take time out from my day or evening to do volunteer work. For the past year I've been tutoring a dyslexic young man in how to read. We work together a few times a week. His family invited me to his graduation.

RD: Do you have to worry about money?

KP: Not since I retired. I have the time to shop wisely now. Would I like more money? You bet. I would like to do more international travel.

RD: What are your future plans?

KP: They keep evolving. Right now I'm still finding out what I want. I realize that I'm probably going to do some writing for magazines and newspapers, maybe a book—that's long been a dream of mine. There's so much to write about. In southern New Jersey, for instance, there is a community of Italians that little has been written about. I plan to interview them.

I recently spent the day with a professional writer who's widely published, and she assured me that I can do much of what she does. I plan to start publishing locally and then branch out nationally.

I think that I would also like renting a stall in an antique facility or actually run my own antique store. The world of antiques is a special kind of world and I love it.

An old friend from graduate school called me and asked if I was interested in some human resources writing for his company. That sounded promising, so we'll get together. Who knows, maybe some day I'll establish a firm specializing in human resources communications.

Right now I'm fifty-five, and what I want is bound to change when I'm sixty or seventy. It's interesting to observe myself changing so much.

RD: What advice would you give other free agents?

KP: Follow your instincts. The possibilities are endless.

* * *

WHAT TO CHARGE

Fee setting used to be the toughest part of being a free agent. Now many professional organizations such as the National Writer's Union provide guidelines on what to charge by the hour or by the project. Also, you can call those in organizations who do the contracting out to get a ballpark idea of what they pay. Many free agents contact the competition, disclose who they are, and ask what their rates are. This usually works well—as long as you're upfront.

Some free agents in demand ignore the market rates and charge what they want, but they usually have unique experience or expertise. One highly credentialed speechwriter in Darien, Connecticut, was said to make $250,000 a year.

Before you start marketing, do the fee-setting homework. What you want to avoid is pricing your services too low. Lowballing gets you a bad reputation. Many assume that those who charge lower-than-average fees are inferior vendors.

GETTING CALLED BACK

Organizations like working with proven entities. If you keep clients happy you can expect repeat business from that organization.

How do you keep clients happy? Go the extra mile. A consumer products company frequently puts vendors on retainer who are able to meet tight deadlines—even if it means working weekends. Some vendors give their clients competitive intelligence; others are well connected and introduce clients to people who may be useful to know.

THANKING CLIENTS

Small gestures count. Maybe it's a book the client should read, or tickets to an Elton John concert, or a memorable lunch. I always find ways to thank my clients for their business. It's a mistake to assume that you are doing such an outstanding job that you don't need to thank the client using your services.

Now You Know...

- The full-time job is disappearing. In its place are professionals who work as free agents.
- Being a free agent has its pros and cons. Whether or not it suits you is a matter of temperament.
- Today the main career concern is being employable, not necessarily in having a full-time job.
- There are a number of ways to start being a free agent. Going to temporary employment agencies is the easiest.
- Often free agents enjoy a high quality of life because they have time to do what they want to do.

4

BOUNCING BACK
FROM A SETBACK

"In a global economy and digital age, we're all going to encounter 'bumps' in the road. I call them transitions. What matters most is not that we got laid off, passed over, or that someone stole our idea. What matters is how we use this experience to refocus our career."

—Richard Taylor, managing partner of the executive search firm Taylor/Rodgers and Associates

What Do I Do?

- Neither my father nor his father had ever lost a job, but I was among the thirteen thousand who got laid off at Raytheon.
- I worked so hard for that promotion, but they passed me over.
- Now it's obvious that I'll never become a CEO.
- I've lost power.
- They talk about my being older.
- I don't understand their humor.

NOT HOW WE PICTURED IT

Since the late 1970s, careers have become unpredictable. That's when the American auto industry started worrying about those little Japanese cars and secretaries started being replaced by personal computers. When I started working in the 1960s I assumed that I would stay with one organization for my entire career, that my talent would be constantly recognized and rewarded, and that I could afford to retire early. That's not how it worked out.

Eight years ago I left a large organization and started my own business. Before that, I never considered myself an entrepreneur. Talent aside, I would sometimes lose clients to hungrier, less-expensive agencies that didn't do a good job. And with educational costs so high for my two sons, I couldn't even think about early retirement. My career was unpredictable.

JOIN THE CLUB

I have plenty of company among professionals whose careers haven't turned out as they expected. A medical doctor told me that she never expected managed care to reduce her power so much. A speechwriter told me that a company let him go after one draft—in the old days he would have had six months to prove himself. A librarian who loves the printed word is spending most of her day supervising the use of the Internet.

THOSE WHO HAVE BOUNCED BACK

What will happen to all those people who are facing new realities? A number of professionals have managed extraordinary recoveries from setbacks. Steve Jobs founded Apple Computer; then he was ousted from the organization by John Sculley. Now Jobs is back at Apple and has restored this institution to profitability. He has also started another successful company that specializes in computer animation.

At Ford, Lee Iacocca assumed he was a shoo-in to succeed Henry Ford II as CEO. Instead, Ford fired him. Iacocca went on to Chrysler and not only saved the company but became a national hero.

At Chrysler, it was rumored that finance honcho Gerald Greenwald thought he would succeed Iacocca as CEO. That didn't happen. Greenwald is now CEO at United Airlines and has gotten high marks from the finance world.

After *Saturday Night Fever*, actor John Travolta faded away, but he's now back making hits. He has redefined himself as a mature actor.

Writer Lee Stringer used to put together brilliant marketing materials, then an addiction to crack grabbed ahold of him. He slept in Grand Central Station and returned soda cans for money. He finally got past his addiction and wrote the provocative book *Grand Central Winter*, which got terrific reviews.

If you take the commuter train from Westchester County or Fairfield County to Manhattan you'll find that many of the seats are filled by people who've picked themselves up after a setback. Some have lost multiple jobs. Some were forced out of their office and into a cubicle. Some lost their business in the recession of 1992. Some assumed that a promotion was in the bag when it wasn't. But they're back in the game now.

Very few of them will say that going through a setback was easy. When we're past forty and our careers take a left turn, it will be one of the toughest in our lives. The challenge is not to panic or slide into self-pity. A setback is just another problem to be solved.

In this chapter we'll examine how we might feel after a setback and what we need to do to get back in the game.

RICHARD TAYLOR, EXECUTIVE RECRUITER

I met Richard Taylor about a year ago. It was obvious that he's a man with twenty-first-century vision and a mission about work issues, so I wanted him to be a part of this book.

Taylor is convinced that our career transitions can be positive experiences, that if handled right, they can propel a career forward or in a better direction. At his executive search firm Taylor/Rodgers and Associates, a boutique specializing in leveraging technology for business gain, Taylor deals with the volatile world of high tech. The companies he serves and the executives he places ride roller coasters of change. He helps them transfer that volatility into an asset.

Before opening his own firm, Taylor was a leading producer at the search firm Korn/Ferry International. His high-tech background includes consulting positions at Real Decisions, a Gartner Group Company, and the Northeast region for Systems Research and Applications Corporation. Like most mature employees and entrepreneurs, Taylor has gone through his own "dark night" in his career.

* * *

INTERVIEW WITH RICHARD TAYLOR

RD: Richard, you have a unique set of credentials. You yourself have been through some rough waters in your career, and you also help thousands of companies and individuals who are forced to look at themselves and ask, "What am I doing?" Could you tell us about your own setback?

RT: Bob, I have learned to call those difficult days transitions. They're setbacks only if you perceive them as setbacks and treat them as such. In this new economy we have to view these events as predictable crises in any career. If you haven't encountered serious obstacles in your career, hey, you're not even trying.

My first transition came when I was a consultant. I was a typical "successful" professional in the New York metropolitan area. I took the train every day to Manhattan from Fairfield County. I was doing well in my work. I liked what I did. My little world was quite perfect. But then the consulting firm was bought, and the organization doing the buying didn't need us incumbents. Talk about shock. I had a family, and I had nothing else lined up in terms of another job. I wasn't prepared to even start *looking* for another job.

From that experience, what I immediately got was the realization that no one can assume continuity in how they make a living. We always have to be thinking ahead to the next job or the next client. That was the early 1990s. This is even more true now. The average job lasts twenty-four to thirty-six months. That's all. Clients aren't loyal anymore. We have to approach making a living as if we're professional athletes who are free agents, or as if we're self-employed.

RD: How long did it take you to land on your feet?

RT: Six months. Six *long* months. Emotionally and financially. In terms of our lifestyles, we have to be prepared for time-outs. This experience taught me to treat my career as any other situation in business. It's a big mistake to just "float" in a profession.

The good news—and this is typical—is that after this transition I got a better job with better pay, and I didn't have to commute into Manhattan. That job lasted about three years, then the company was bought and it was bye-bye again, only this time I had the mind-set that I had to take care of myself. So, my mind was open to new possibilities.

Since my first encounter with unemployment I had been doing volunteer work with others in the same boat. I coached them on everything from how to deal with their families to what not to say to an interviewer. I loved this work, and it showed. A number of people said, "Richard, you have a passion for helping people change professionally. Why not do that for a living?" I listened, and I decided to make a career change. I was able to find a position as an executive recruiter in one of the top recruiting firms in the world. I now knew how to handle change strategically. After spending some time with that firm, I decided to open my own company, which bears the stamp of my own vision and mission.

RD: I guess the big question readers have is: Can we *prevent* setbacks?

RT: I'm convinced that isn't a productive way of thinking. Transitions will happen. That's a new fact of life. The transition can come in the form of losing a job, getting passed over for a promotion, somebody stealing an idea from you, losing your power, or your approach no longer being fashionable. In my experience with companies and individuals, those upsets really can't be prevented. If you're working at Merrill Lynch and the company decides to lay off 3,500 employees, how could you have prevented that? What matters is not the nature of the experience but how we manage it.

However, we can keep improving how we're positioned in an organization or how our own business is positioned. We can also reduce the odds that we will be victimized if we don't act "old." We need to be in good physical shape. If we are in good shape and we won't shuffle around; we'll walk with direction. In addition, we need to stay fresh in our thinking. We also should show initiative. Without anyone asking us, we should be providing ideas for improving operations or products.

RD: I know what you mean. I have an employee in the organization who's nearly eighty, and he keeps his job because he has tremendous initiative. He's always suggesting ways to do things better.

RT: I can't emphasize it enough: We are all free agents. It's up to us to position ourselves to do as well as we can in the marketplace.

RD: What's the "to-do" list for a transition? Many people will be losing their jobs in the coming years. What are the next steps?

RT: The key thing is to not panic. In sorting out your career opportunities, you need time. For those who don't have savings, they have to buy that time with survival-type jobs or freelancing. One of the biggest mistakes in a transition is to assume that an opportunity presented to you, such as a job, is your only and last opportunity and that you must grab it.

Handling a career crises is hard at any age, but it's harder for those over forty. We have to treat what we are going through as a process. As with death, there will be predictable stages of feeling. We will go through shock, denial, bargaining, anger, acceptance, and moving forward. During this process, we'll probably need help. We can frequently get that free of charge. In the county in which I live, for example, the churches and self-help groups provide everything from emotional counseling about what we really want to job leads. Those support systems can be lifelines. You can get information about such support systems from the local newspaper, word of mouth, or a social work agency like the United Way.

Another challenge during a transition is keeping optimistic. I'll see lots of signs of depression in professionals who are looking for new opportunities. Fortunately, the medical community now offers excellent treatment for depression. That's a big advance for all of us. Depression clouds judgment and makes us present ourselves poorly. Often we can go right to our family doctor for a prescription for antidepressant medication.

Technology is another major resource for us during transitions. The Internet features plenty of goodies, ranging from job openings to advice on how to approach interview questions. On-line services provide information about companies and industries. That research is a must-do before going to an interview.

Another key resource is our families. There used to be "funny" stories about executives who got fired but still went into Manhattan every day in a suit, pretending that they have a job. Concealing what's going on in our careers from our family is a disservice to them and to ourselves. When transitions take place, families can get pretty scared. They feel that they're powerless, that they're in the passenger seat and have no control over where the car is headed or at what speed. Informing families about our game plan helps neutralize that fear. We also have to let them know that we need emotional support—but not judgments. It's up to us to let our families know how they can be most useful. Those going through this process can also help themselves by analyzing how other people our age have gotten through career transitions. At Disney, CEO Michael Eisner pushed out a number of executives. How are they doing? What did they do right and what could they have handled better?

* * *

WHY WE DREAD SETBACKS

We're from a generation that grew up being pretty hard on those who had setbacks. On *Father Knows Best*, Jim Anderson never lost his insurance job or agonized about a power struggle in the office. Ben Casey only had to worry about his patients, not if the hospital would stay solvent. The Lone Ranger called all the shots and could expect loyalty from his staff of one. Our national psyche wasn't conditioned to deal with failure.

THE STIGMA OF FAILURE

In the mid-1970s, much of the academic market collapsed in the United States. It was heartbreaking. Many of the best and the brightest who were studying for doctorates so they could teach in universities couldn't get academic jobs. When they tried to make the transition to business or government, many potential employers gave them a rough time because they assumed that these people had failed in their previous careers. Those who got laid off in America during the recession of 1974 were also treated like second-class citizens. Potential employers grilled them about why they were let go. What had they done "wrong"?

Back then, career progress was supposed to be linear. From the time we left school to the time we retired, nothing "bad" was supposed to happen. Those who did get knocked around kept it quiet.

Setbacks were also verboten in America because of our Calvinist heritage. As John Ward states in *Song of the Phoenix: The Hidden Rewards of Failure*, we were socialized to expect good material things to happen to good people. If we were getting pummeled by circumstances, we were probably not living a righteous life.[1] In short, bad career changes only happened to bad people. Many thought that Frank Sinatra's career took a nosedive because he was "bad" or arrogant or not nice to his wife.

THE FADING TABOO OF FAILURE

The stigma associated with having setbacks is declining. Since the late 1980s, millions of corporate jobs have disappeared. There's a glut in just about every profession, ranging from law to nursing. In a global economy, anyone can catch the Asian or Russian flu. It's also being recognized that people will let go of a good job to have a better quality of life.

As Richard Taylor pointed out, helping one deal with professional setbacks is now part of the infrastructure of a community. In affluent Fairfield County, the newspaper the *Advocate* carries listings for support groups for the unemployed.

FAILURE AS A RITE OF PASSAGE

Unfortunately, it's still part of the American mind-set to truly believe that if we're shrewd enough or talented enough, setbacks won't happen to us. That belief has to go. A major setback or transition has to be an accepted rite of passage. It's boot camp for developing into an enduring professional. At General Electric, which has been ahead of the curve for about two decades, new managers aren't taken seriously until they've been beaten up some. It's my take that in running your own business you're not a proven entrepreneur until you've lost your major client—and survived.

One day soon, I predict, the first thing a potential employer will ask a job candidate is, "What kind of setbacks have you had and how did you handle them?" If I were a venture capitalist I wouldn't lend money to entrepreneurs who hadn't been kicked around.

BE GENTLE WITH YOURSELF

Every day, some former or passed-over executive comes into my office and beats himself up. One told me, "If only I hadn't gone to that food company—I knew that it just had been taken over. I should have anticipated layoffs." Come on, how well can any of us read the future?

Another displaced executive beat himself up because twenty years ago he hadn't had the foresight to major in business. The reality is that many liberal-arts graduates do as well as those with business degrees. If we blame ourselves for decisions we made years ago, we're just wasting time. For most of us, the decisions we made back then were the right decisions for us at that time. Suppose we had decided to work for a medical degree before managed care became a reality? At the time it was probably a good decision. Now managed care has changed everything. But what use is it for medical doctors to beat themselves up about a decision that made sense at the time?

I tell executives I counsel that it's grandiose for them to take the full blame for the circumstances in which they find themselves. It's far wiser to stop playing the blame-myself game and to move forward.

Winners in the professional world are gentle with themselves. No matter what mistakes they have made, they recognize that mistakes are history and that they should focus on the present and future. In her autobiography *Personal History*, Katharine Graham explains how she was able to go from being a corporate wife to the head of a media empire. Her secret was that she didn't allow her mistakes to bother her too much.[2]

FORGIVE THOSE #*##*#***

Nothing dates us like a resentment that is five, ten, or fifteen years old. There was a man on the commuter train whom we nicknamed Gulf Oil. Although Gulf had been taken over by Chevron and was no longer in existence, the man still ranted and raved about a particular boss he had there. That boss, he claimed, passed him over for a promotion twice. No one took this man seriously. He was stuck in the past.

Forgiving those who we think did us in is smart policy. Once we forgive those culprits, they won't be running around in our heads anymore and we'll be free to focus all our attention on the present and future.

Forgiving the rascals also makes sense. It's rare that we can really discern who did what to whom and why. For several years a woman resented a superior who had spoken to her about her drinking problem. She thought that he had a lot of nerve, especially since he also liked to wet his whistle. As a result, she left the company and bad-mouthed that boss for years. Only later, when she was in Alcoholics Anonymous for a few months, did she realize that he was doing a caring thing. He hadn't reported her problem to anyone else in the company; he was approaching her as a friend.

How can we come to forgive those who might have done us harm? We have to realize that we all make mistakes. Superiors, clients, and colleagues have all made mistakes in dealing with me, and I with them. Some of those mistakes cost me money and angst. So what? Am I okay now? Yes, so I can let it go.

CALL IN FAVORS

This is the age of networking. We get the most help from other people, but we have to let them know that we need help. Many people owe us a favor or two. A neighbor who used to take care of our house while we were away got laid off in a downsizing but never told us. I could have helped him.

I know that it's hard to make that call to someone announcing that things aren't going so well. We're embarrassed. We might be in shock. But, we don't have to call the very day we get bad news. We can wait for a few days or even a week and sort out who we feel comfortable calling.

There are all kinds of help we can get from people once we call them. They can give us information about certain companies or jobs. They can let us use their name when we're contacting possible employers or clients. They can actually set up lunches or coffees at which we can meet people. They can brief us as to what is expected in their profession in case we want to switch. They can give us constructive criticism about our résumés or how we're coming across. One man put on probation at his company called a colleague at another company for whom he had done a number of favors and asked him for help. The other man talked with him for hours and persuaded him to see a psychotherapist. The man is now doing well.

TAKE AN INVENTORY OF YOUR STRENGTHS

Other people told Richard Taylor he would be good in recruiting work. More often, we're not that lucky. We have to find our strengths on our own.

Strengths come in all forms. In *The Power Game*, Hedrick Smith notes that many different things can empower a person professionally. For example, he points out that confidence is power, self-assurance is power, credibility is power.[3] Those traits can have as much impact on our career—or more—as an MBA from Harvard Business School.

None of this is new. Way back in the 1930s, interactional pioneer Dale Carnegie taught his public-speaking students that social skills are prerequisites to success. In *How to Win Friends and Influence People*, he described everything a professional needs to do when interacting in the work place.[4]

What is new about these social traits is that the work world is taking them seriously. It's no longer the best engineer who gets to be director, it's the engineer who knows how to get people to cooperate. Social skills—or as they are sometimes called, emotional intelligence—are now a clear career asset, so you should list those characteristics in our "strength" column. Make the list comprehensive. A mother who was good at getting her kids to stop fighting might find a new career in conflict resolution.

In addition to this "soft side" of our strengths portfolio are our knowledge base, skills, and experience. One woman who had worked on her high school newspaper answered an ad for an intern on a local newspaper. Within a few years she had navigated her way, mostly through networking, to work on a national publication.

After you write down this raw data, organize it into categories. There will be at least one category for each direction your career could take. For example, a writer may have two categories for his career: "Keep writing" and "Move up to management." By sorting out your options like this, you'll learn where you have the most horsepower. Then you can match that strength with the opportunities out there.

When a public relations person was downsized from a food company she did a strength inventory. That's how she realized she had what it took to open her own business. She did a market review to find out if her services were needed. It was a match.

FIX THE WEAK AREAS

A manager at a major telecommunications company lost a big job because she was weak on social skills. A sympathetic client advised that she take a Dale Carnegie seminar, but she didn't want to spend the money. She hasn't yet regained her momentum.

Deficits come in all kinds of packages—I was overweight by one hundred pounds, and had to lose that weight to become more effective with clients. A sixty-five-year-old man was out of work and had to learn how to use a word processor. An entrepreneur who wasn't getting enough business had to move her firm from Hartford, Connecticut, to Stamford, Connecticut.

Some weak areas can't be fixed. General Electric CEO Jack Welch had a speech impediment, which he compensated for by making what he said so provocative. A fifty-year-old woman in Troy, Michigan, with a pronounced Brooklyn accent went to a speech therapist to "reduce a regional accent." The remedial treatment was too hard for her to do at her age. She compensated by moving back to New York, where her accent didn't stand out as much. At forty, one woman who finished college was very shy, and public-speaking courses and Prozac didn't help. She decided that the best place for her to work would be a library, and she went on to get a master's degree in information science.

When you're having trouble fixing your weak areas, try the Serenity Prayer: pray for the wisdom to know what you can change and then change it; what you can't change, find a way to get around it or accept it.

THINK OUT-OF-THE-BOX

A magazine editor was passed over for a promotion. He could have switched to another publication, but instead he approached his problem with out-of-the-box thinking. He realized that he knew a great deal about the communications industry, so he started a business specializing in finding, screening, and placing temporary help in communications for a certain geographic area.

For about a decade, a stay-at-home mom managed her family's investment portfolio. When her marriage collapsed, she initially thought that all she could do was secretarial work. Then she discussed her situation with an old college friend who was in public relations. The friend advised her to take a few finance courses and then try to get a job in investor relations in a public relations agency. Today she is a partner in an investor relations firm.

A woman who had spent her life in ladies' fashion retail was able to transfer some of those skills to establish a real estate brokerage firm dealing with restaurants. What she had to learn was all the due diligence needed to set up such a business. A man who had taught high school for years made the transition to sales; he realized he had been "pitching" all his life. In his new profession he sold telecommunication systems. A superintendent of a condo complex took all he knew about building management and bought up property when the price was low as an investment.

PASS IT ON

Once we are back on our feet there are many ways we can pass or give back to others what we've gained. Defeated presidential candidate Bob Dole went on national television and explained what he had learned from losing. Actress Patty Duke, once her mental illness had been diagnosed and properly treated, became an advocate for those with similar problems. The same was true of the late publisher Frances Lear. In my community, executives who've been through the wringer with job changes mentor those who are just starting to feel the turbulence. Many of my associates know that if they're thinking about making the transition from corporate life to entrepreneur, I'll share what I have learned.

Passing it on helps keep fresh in our mind what we've been through. That helps us appreciate what we have now.

A FRESH START

But a transition from one line of work, or city, or country, to another doesn't necessarily mean a fresh start. In our interconnected global village it is almost impossible to begin all over again and not bump into someone from our past.

Rather than expecting a new start, it's much more productive if we take the positive attitude that we have certainly learned a lot from our previous experiences, no matter how turbulent they might have been. Experience is experience, and all of it is worthwhile. Many Watergate figures such as Charles Colson built new careers after that crisis. Ex-prisoner Michael Milken, the Wall Street whiz, has a new career in cancer education and prevention. I expect wild child Mike Tyson to have another career after serving his jail term.

The point is: Don't waste energy trying to run away from the past. Use it.

PEACE

It is our responsibility to come to terms with the demons that were unleashed by a setback. Running won't bring peace. One man I know has come to peace with his past by assessing how much he had learned from his negative experiences. At one corporation, he was relocated to Siberia. He left that job and got a better one. Then he was fired. He was also fired from the next job. It took all that to push this security-minded man to open his own business. Since he's become an entrepreneur no one has fired him.

SUCCESS BY STAYING IN PLACE

There's a lot of rhetoric about relocation to places like North Carolina or changing professions after going through some type of career crisis—that it's supposed to bring better odds for success. Actually, those who make the greatest career gains after a setback are those who stay put—but fine-tune their modus operandi. A man I know lost two big corporate jobs within a few years. He humbly asked people what he was doing wrong. He repackaged himself for the consulting world and is now making top dollar. Nothing else in his life has changed.

On the other hand, another entrepreneur I've worked with lost her business in 1994 and took a job in another city. That meant two adjustments: to a job working for someone else and to a new city. She quickly moved back to her original city and opened a different type of business.

The grass may be different in another town or profession, but it isn't necessarily greener.

PREPARING FOR THE NEXT CRISIS

I agree with Richard Taylor: There is rarely a way to prevent a setback. The wheels of the machine that demand lower costs or are moving toward a merger usually roll our way—no matter what we do. However, we can be well positioned when the setback happens.

The best offensive strategy is networking. Entrepreneur Harvey Mackay wrote a book called *Dig Your Well Before You Need It*, in which he predicts that one night we're going to wake up around 2:00 A.M. and realize that we need some kind of help—maybe advice, maybe a job connection, maybe a lunch in our honor. Who are we going to call to get that help? That's what Mackay means about digging your well: develop a network *before* you need it. Do favors for lots of different people. And read my chapter on networking.

Another important strategy is to avoid being a victim. If we keep up-to-date in our appearance, word choices, references, knowledge base, and skills, we're less of a target. We all know what happens to the older worker who keeps complaining about how hard the new software is. He goes in the first wave of cuts—and who would ever consider him for a promotion?

The third strategy is to handle money wisely. The more money we have available when a crisis happens the more leverage we have in seeking our options. I've seen former Wall Street "Masters of the Universe" bag groceries in the supermarket after they were canned because they had been living from paycheck to paycheck.

Now You Know...

- Setbacks happen to everyone. What matters is not the setback but how we handle it.
- Setbacks can be defining moments, opportunities for growth.
- When we have a setback, we should be gentle with ourselves, forgive those who might have harmed us, call in our favors on the network, take an inventory of our strengths, fix our weaknesses, think out-of-the-box, and give back to society.
- There probably isn't such a thing as a fresh start.
- Be prepared for the next setback by networking.

5

WHEN OUR VALUES CHANGE

*Most of us will arrive at some point in our lives when the world
with which we are most familiar no longer works for us.*
—Caroline Myss, Ph.D., *Why People Don't Heal*

What Do I Do?

- If I didn't have one more kid to put through school, I could think about quitting my job and taking a year off.
- Everything that used to be important to me just doesn't matter as much now.
- Does this sound crazy? Here I am, forty-seven, and I want to adopt a child.
- I'm fifty-two and haven't made the big time.
- In my career I've accomplished everything I wanted to, but I'm not happy at work.

WHAT'S IMPORTANT NOW?

It's often said that values are the glue that holds us together—as individuals and as a society. When those values change, as they're bound to in middle age, our equilibrium can go out the window.

An investor relations specialist I'll call Rick had his day in the sun during an attempted takeover at an energy company. Everyone was consulting him, but the company lost—and was taken over. Rick's job disappeared and he lost his belief in business values. He then decided to do public relations for a nonprofit firm, but he didn't fit in. He still hasn't found his way.

In the professional world there are now millions of Ricks. I'm one of them. Twice I went through a rough patch when my old values just didn't match the person I was becoming. One time was when I made the shift from corporate life to being an entrepreneur. The next was when I became a father late in life. The good news is that although Rick is still struggling, most of us do get through the periods when we question just about everything. In this chapter we'll look at changing values and how we can come out on the other side stronger—and happier.

VALUES

Values have been getting lots of attention lately. If you use the Infoseek search engine on the Internet and key in *personal values*, you'll find more than nine million Web site entries.

Fast Company magazine writer Harriet Rubin explains that it's lethal to base one's total self-esteem on professional accomplishments.[1] Successful people are beginning to look at the values that are motivating them.

In *Hungry Spirit*, Charles Handy, who was one of the first to write about the growth of contingent workers, points out that many of us no longer find the values of capitalism enough. Handy asserts that the developed world is discovering that we need more than money and profits. Work has to be meaningful.[2]

There's a simplification movement afoot in which people are struggling to live by their core values while purging their lives of what's unnecessary. To do this, they're willing to cut their earnings to improve their quality of life. These simplifiers are sometimes called dumpster divers, since they'll raid trash piles to save money.

Much of the controversy about "Monicagate" was about values. The public wanted to know: What values influenced the president's decision to do what he did? And what about Monica Lewinsky's values? Is it okay for a young woman to have a fling with a married man?

In business there's a renewed interest in manners, and that's really about values. The bookstores are full of guides to etiquette. Manners, stresses etiquette expert Letitia Baldrige, are about how people treat one another. There's more to the workplace than getting work out; executives are also responsible for the morale of the office, and morale is a result of how people perceive they are being treated. An example of values in the workplace is using *we* rather than *I*—that is, acting in the best interests of all rather than just yourself.

THE MIDLIFE CRISIS

This period of questioning our values is sometimes called a midlife crisis. In *New Passages: Mapping Your Life Across Time*, social commentator Gail Sheehy called this period of transition a passage.[3] I like to think of the time we devote to questioning our values as a sabbatical from life as usual. Former Pepsi and Apple executive John Sculley seemed to enjoy backing away from business and taking stock of his values. In *Odyssey*, he describes some of that journey.[4]

Actually, most of us take some time for reflection whenever we're thinking about the next step. If we want to try new things, we usually have to take a break from business as usual. Before Lee Iacocca became "savior" of Chrysler, he was out of work and had lots of time to think. Before Jesus started his public life, he withdrew and meditated. Companies planning major changes usually hold retreats for their executives.

With so much in the work world, more and more of us will be simply stopping—and thinking. That could last a day or a year. During this period of questioning we might rent a van and tour the country or take some courses at the community college. But the end result can be amazing. A writer took a few months off to figure out what she wanted to write about. She was tired of corporate work. She found a new writing career in the "inspirational" market. Actor John Travolta dropped out for a while and came back stronger than ever. Over time Jimmy Carter was able to make the transition from "president who didn't get reelected" to ambassador for peace.

I've seen too many outstanding professionals fall off the cliff into nothingness because they didn't take the time to stop and think.

WHAT WE'RE SO UPSET ABOUT

So many of our questions about our values have to do with proportion. At one time work was more important to many of us than social life, spiritual awareness, or creativity. Then one day, work became less important, and that change in proportion upset us. We may have felt naked and disoriented or wondered if people were laughing at us. We might have found ourselves doing "foolish" things, such as blabbing to the person next to us on the train about our feelings about work. Management consultant Joan Lloyd sees our personal values as what primarily motivates us to do what we do, to make the choices we make, to love the people we love. Her list of values that might strongly influence us follows.

- The need to accomplish or master something
- The desire to make progress in our careers by climbing the ladder or increasing earnings
- The excitement of adventure
- Seeing competitiveness as a good thing
- Making a difference in society
- Cooperating with others to achieve a goal
- Being creative in problem solving
- The need to be financially secure
- The need to amass wealth
- The "soft values" of life, such as friendship, good family relationships, and inner peace
- The need for intangibles such as freedom
- Seeking good health and fitness
- A sense of belonging
- The need for fun
- Spiritual yearning
- The need to be right
- The desire for power or recognition[5]

To Lloyd's list I would add some values I've found to be big influences on my clients, friends, and colleagues:

- The need to compensate for events in the past
- The need to give back to society or a feeling of discomfort about success
- The desire for change
- The wish to heal
- The hunger for dignity

THEN AND NOW

Look over these lists. Then, get out a sheet of paper and divide it into two columns. One column represents how important each of the values were to you five years ago. The second represents how important each are now. Indicate the importance of each on a scale of one to ten.

By doing this exercise you can see which of these values have lost importance to you, and what counts right now. Many of us will probably have to do such an exercise several times in our lives. We're living longer and there's so much change going on in the world. We're bound to become undone any number of times. The challenge is to change, once we know what we want.

HELP OUT THERE

The biggest mistake we can make during this transition is to try to go it alone. Some of us assume that if we don't go for help no one will know how much we're suffering. Wrong. In my experience, it's usually pretty obvious when we're wrestling with our values. Fortunately, there's plenty of help available and much of it is free or low cost.

With all the help available to us, there is no reason why we should allow a midlife crisis to ruin our career or destroy a relationship. Also, it's easier to go on this journey with help from others.

BOOKS

It seems that just about everyone over the age of forty has written a book sharing their insights about being "older." New on the market are books by former president Jimmy Carter and television personality Hugh Downs. Remember when entertainer Bill Cosby's book on aging was a daring act? There will be plenty more books coming out. Some thinkers such as Caroline Myss don't target their writing specifically for those over forty, but the kind of pain they discuss, such as not letting old wounds heal, is directly applicable to us.[6]

PSYCHOTHERAPISTS

Psychotherapists offer specialized therapy for people over forty. When I was starting out in life, psychotherapy was geared primarily to the young, people who had enough of life left to apply what they had learned in the "talking cure" which usually took many years. The ideal client then was a YIV—young, intelligent, and verbal.

Now that we're living longer, we, too, can profit from talking with a therapist, and most of us will have many years to use the insight we get. Basically, a therapist serves as a mirror for us to see ourselves more clearly. Depending on her orientation, she will listen, but she may or may not give advice.

There are all kinds of ways to pay for this. Your medical insurance might cover it, and some clinics have sliding fees, based on income. There are training facilities for mental health students that serve the public at low cost. You can also try bartering, for example, trading your marketing or accounting expertise for the therapist's time.

How can you find the right therapist? Just about every community has a central mental health clearing house listed in the Yellow Pages under "Mental Health." There is also word of mouth. Or, you can shop around. Visit a few therapists to find out who is the best fit for you.

Psychotherapy can be especially helpful for those whose midlife crisis mimics adolescence. In adolescence, we're supposed to create a separate identity for ourselves, break away from the ways of childhood and decide what's important to us. Many of us do exactly the same things in our midlife turmoil, so by working with a therapist we might be able to keep a lid on any acting out we might do.

SPIRITUALITY

Spiritual groups ranging from Buddhists to Wiccans are attracting more and more middle-age people. One of my vendors looked into the

Quakers, the Unitarians, and a few Pentecostal religions. She decided, though, to return to the Roman Catholic church, which she had left in adolescence. When she told me about this, the image of Woody Allen shopping around for a religion during his crisis in *Hannah and Her Sisters* jumped into my mind.

Back in the mid-1980s, when *Hannah* came out, searching for a faith was still a sort of joke. Now we're taking it a little more seriously. That's because research is showing that a belief system can change our whole world. The *New York Times* recently carried an article entitled "Placebos Prove So Powerful Even Experts Are Surprised" in which hard-nosed scientists concede that what we believe can shape the results we get.[7] If we believe that there is a benevolent deity looking out for us, we might sail through a job search. If we believe, as Wiccans do, that the good we do is returned threefold, we will do good and expect good things to come our way. And they will. Beliefs really do shape our destiny.

HEALERS

Many people I know around my age consult with all kinds of healers who practice what is often referred to as "alternative medicine." Healing has gone mainstream. A level-headed government employee retired from the Social Security Administration in Baltimore and did freelance investigative government work. She hated it. Then she tried opening up a consignment shop. No money. She thought about becoming a mediator but didn't want to take one more course in her life. By word of mouth, she got the name of a European couple who healed minds and bodies. They only charged $60 for two hours, and she saw them for about twelve sessions. She's now getting experience in freelance writing for everything from magazines to public relations agencies. She swears that her new direction—at fifty-five years of age—came from healers.

Of course, some healers are charlatans. The best way to find the right healer is by word of mouth. Some people have luck finding healers through their churches. There are also classified ads in publications and on the Internet. Interview healers over the phone—before you pay.

MOVE THAT BODY

Exercise is a mood changer. In Stamford, Connecticut, the Jewish Community Center has special physical activities for older people, and those who attend are among the spryest in the town.

If someone you know is going through a divorce or a job search, the best thing you can do for them is give them a month's membership to a gym. Moving our bodies distracts us from the negatives in life.

FRIENDS—INCLUDING THOSE IN CYBERSPACE

We can talk with each other—in person, on the phone, or in cyberspace. Older colleague after older colleague confide to me that they are having problems putting in the usual fourteen-hour day; their energy level is not what it was when they were in their forties. From talking with me and others they usually learn to pace themselves in new ways. Instead of being a hard-charger all day they now take breaks, and somehow they piece together a workday long enough to get everything done. A confused fifty-three-year old graphic artist announced to her friends that she was going to retire. Her friends got her to see that she was a type A personality and would always need to work, at least for emotional reasons. Thanks to input from friends, she's downsized her retirement dream to semi-retirement.

Friends know us well. They know when we're lying to ourselves, even when we don't.

GENERATION X

Another way to make it through rough waters is to understand different kinds of values. That helps us to see our own values more clearly. In writing my last book, I interviewed hundreds of Generation Xers, many of whom told me that they don't see making a living as a vocation or "sacred calling." That led me to realize that I approach my career too seriously, and that was a big help to me.

A PSYCHOLOGIST REFLECTS ON AGING

Patricia Cardinale, Ph.D., has been practicing psychotherapy for more than two decades. She started her career as an intern at Long

Island Jewish Medical Center, working with senior citizens on an outpatient basis. The hospital's programs for the aging were ahead of their time. Dr. Cardinale handled everything from assessment of cognitive skills to marital therapy in which the entire family was involved. Those who asked, "Why do marital therapy with a seventy-year old?" were told that if marriage was a problem with the elderly, the staff addressed it. During her internship, Dr. Cardinale found out that the elderly had the same long-term learning ability as younger people.

Dr. Cardinale rounded out her skills working with troubled teenagers who were in a residential facility. She is currently working with a general population, and an increasing number of her clients are over forty. She frequently uses technology in her work and has published papers on using technology to eliminate writer's block.

* * *

INTERVIEW WITH DR. PATRICIA CARDINALE

RD: How do psychologists like yourself define *aging*?

PC: That keeps changing. It used to be that we considered someone who was about sixty-five to be old. Now, even in the research literature, sixty-five to seventy is considered young-old and seventy-five to ninety is considered old-old, based on life expectancy. What we're seeing is that the aged is not a homogenous group. There are big differences between, say, sixty-five and seventy-four and between seventy-four and ninety. There's a lot of research taking place right now with seventy-four to ninety-year-olds.

Also, we have to remember that there are not only differences between broad age categories, there are also many individual differences between people. One person may go through a midlife crisis at thirty-eight while another will go through it in his seventies. The same holds true for "losses." Some individuals may retain an excellent memory until they die at ninety-four, while others may experience cognitive decay in their fifties.

RD: From these differences, I guess we could infer that employers shouldn't stereotype all workers over forty as the same.

PC: No. There are many differences in how we age.

RD: In Psychology 101 at Notre Dame I learned that life consisted of
      necessary and predictable stages, and in each stage there were
      certain developmental "tasks" to accomplish. For example, when
      we're very little, some of the developmental tasks are to learn to
      walk and talk. What are we "responsible for" accomplishing as we
      age?

PC: Aging is a stage of life. Many theorists have written about this, and
      there is now a lot of literature on the developmental tasks of aging.
      Here, again, we must remember that no two people age alike. So no
      two people will be on the same "schedule."

      One major developmental job of aging is to come to grips with
      the fact that we will die—not just Joe across the street, but
      ourselves. We have to face our mortality. Once we do that we will
      take care of the practical things like creating a will, establishing an
      estate that will shield our family from taxes, deciding on burial
      versus cremation, those sorts of things.

RD: Now I understand something. One of my vendors is about sixty.
      She's been working hard to find a place for her animals once she
      dies, making decisions about what to leave to whom. She has even
      specified the choreography of her funeral. Now I see that that's
      what she's *supposed to be* doing at her age.

PC: Yes. That's easier to do now than it was thirty years ago, when
      discussing death was taboo. But facing mortality is still a difficult
      subject, and it might take time to get to it.

RD: What are the other tasks of aging?

PC: Another big job is to accept whatever limits our health has placed
      on us. If our body can't endure a fourteen-hour day anymore,
      maybe we have to accept that we need a less demanding job. Some
      people will experience few limits, though. There are political
      figures like Robert Byrd who seem to sustain the same pace they
      had for years. But for the rest of us there will be decisions to make
      about what kind of work we can do now and how active a lifestyle
      we can have. Two of my female friends both told me that once they
      hit fifty, they could only do one social thing a day. Those over forty
      might find that they can only work during the week and not
      socialize.

      A third major task is to integrate your life for yourself, to find meaning. If you want to move ahead, it's useful to weave a life history for yourself, to bring together all the pieces so that they make sense. Review what led up to your decision about your career, how that decision influenced other ones, who had input on your professional choice, and what social connections came about as a result of this choice. Talk this out with someone or write it up. To get information that is foggy, contact family members or other people from that time in your life. Of course, you will have some regrets in looking over your life, but don't stay there. Focus primarily on the good things and you'll be able to move on.

Another major task is to enthusiastically embrace new things in your life. You may love to work, but the only work you're able to get at eighty years old may be volunteer work. Go for it. Freud said that love and work are important. I agree. I would also add play. We don't have to give up work as we age, it just might take a different form. This idea of embracing the new is key. Research shows that people who age successfully remain active and aren't isolated. Work is a great opportunity to socialize.

Another necessary task is to come to terms with our dreams. A lawyer might have dreamed of becoming a Supreme Court justice since college. Now he's in his seventies and hasn't developed a national reputation. And his health is just so-so. His task is to accept that odds are he will not become a Supreme Court justice. However, he *can* search his life history to figure out what led up to that dream. Did he want to make a difference in the law? Well, he may have already made a difference and he should congratulate himself for that. Or, he can still make a difference. He can teach a basic course in law in a low-income neighborhood. He can write a provocative article, or mentor young law students.

RD: Coming to terms with our dreams is very interesting. I knew a man who was on a popular soap opera for years but never forgave himself for not having done "serious" acting, as in Shakespearean plays. That ate away at him. In his early sixties he died of a heart attack. Could friends have helped him realize that he was a tremendous success?

PC: The point in moving forward is to be positive about the past and optimistic about what's to come. Talking things out with others is very helpful, and friends can help us by emphasizing the positive.

RD: In many of the things I read about aging, there's usually something there about getting a sense of peace. Is that just wishful thinking, or do we really achieve a new type of peace within ourselves?

PC: If we do all the developmental tasks that we are supposed to do, such as accepting limits, then we can find peace—not the kind of peace that has us just lulling about, but the peace that frees us to move forward. This peace is a motivator in our lives. It propels us forward.

RD: In the workplace, I see that older workers who think "young" survive layoffs and even get promoted. How can we learn to think "young"?

PC: We have to work at it. That's because our environment or our background has sent us negative messages about aging. Thinking "young," in a nutshell, is optimism. It's seeing the glass as half full rather than half empty. It's restructuring the messages in our head.

There's a helpful book, *Learned Optimism*, which shows us that we can reframe our thinking patterns. We can interrupt that circle in our head that says, "You're having a middle-age crisis. That means that you're not young, that you're old and useless." We can reprogram how we perceive the pain we might be going through, and changing our thoughts can change our behavior. It's all interconnected.

We can get help in changing how we think by going to group therapy. Its members will flag us when we are being negative. Another way is to do volunteer work. That will change our perception that older people are useless.

This is a lifetime job because negativity comes naturally. We have to keep interrupting that circle.

Incidentally, getting a pet can help us become more positive. Pets feed so many of our human needs. The pet doesn't have to be a big dog, it can be a goldfish or a ferret.

RD: I heard that when going through a crisis exercise helps a lot.

PC: New research is showing that exercise has enormous impact—and not only on our moods. It has also proved that exercise improves cognitive functioning. In addition, exercise can help us become less preoccupied with ourselves by helping us to stop dwelling on what's wrong with our lives.

RD: I read in the *New York Times* that an increasing number of people my age are seeing psychotherapists. Why is this happening?

PC: For a number of reasons. Sometimes a family member, usually a younger person, encourages an older relative to be diagnosed by a mental health worker. When the older person comes, he soon finds he enjoys therapy and is getting a lot out of it. Older people get so much out of our sessions because they know they have limited time and want to make the most of it. Often someone who's older will find out that a friend her age is talking with a psychotherapist. When she sees a change in that friend, she'll consider trying it. In addition, there's now some kind of insurance coverage for psycho-therapy, so older people can get this service without sacrificing their savings.

RD: If you could give a person in crisis one message, what would it be?

PC: Balance. Depression, anxiety, and loneliness are frequently the consequences of a lack of balance in our lives. The retiree is going to become depressed if she has no work in her life. I say find a volunteer job. Find balance.

* * *

THOSE WHO MAKE IT THROUGH

From what Dr. Cardinale says, getting older seems like an extraordi-nary opportunity for growth—if we're willing to clean out our closets and make changes. So many people have come into their own as they've aged. The ones whose growth I most admire are entrepreneur Ted Turner, actress Liz Taylor, former president Jimmy Carter, Watergate reporter Bob Woodward, and IBM Chief Executive Officer Lou Gerstner.

HOW ARE WE DOING?

How do we know that we're making progress in redefining ourselves? We'll see it in the faces of our family, colleagues, and friends. They'll be more relaxed around us. We'll sleep better and won't tire so easily. We'll handle upsets with more grace and dignity. Career shocks will merely be problems to be solved, not the end of the world.

In *Why People Don't Heal*, Caroline Myss, Ph.D., says that there are signals that indicate we are becoming more self-aware—and therefore more ready to make changes in our life. Here are some of the signals Dr. Myss sees as important:

- Growing dissatisfaction
- A sense of isolation
- A feeling that you can't return to who you were, even though you don't know who you're becoming
- The emergence of expertise and skills you didn't know you had (for instance, the engineer who finds he's good at counseling)
- The willingness to operate on your own time clock rather than society's
- An interest in the "soft side" of life, such as spirituality, nature, or the luxury of time alone[8]

PROGNOSIS

Most of us are probably going to make it. There's now too much help available for us to hurt our careers because we're temporarily confused.

Now You Know...

- If we're getting older, we're probably going to question our values. That turmoil can temporarily undo us.
- Help is available in many forms.
- As we age, there are certain "jobs" we have to get done, such as finding meaning in our life.
- Work will keep us balanced. "Work" doesn't necessarily mean for pay.
- With all the resources out there, we're bound to land on our feet.

6

STAYING SMART

Smart is no longer a destination: it's a journey.
　　　—Lisa Marshall, "Why Smart Organizations Don't Learn"

What Do I Do?

- I don't feel so smart anymore.
- I'm considering going for an MBA—and I'm forty-five years old.
- I'm self-employed. Should I spend my own money on courses?
- I resent all the time I have to put in just to keep up with my field.

LEARNING, LEARNING, LEARNING

There's a social revolution going on. Men and women our age are aggressively going after learning opportunities of all kinds. Not since the GI Bill have there been so many adults taking advantage of learning, and I'm convinced that the seventy-six million baby boomers who are entering middle age will change forever what the world thinks about the older professional and our ability to learn new things. Psychologists are observing that people over forty are able to change very rapidly once they realize that change is necessary. After all, unlike teenagers, who frequently resist change, we know that we have only a finite amount of time left.

84

RETOOLING

Community college has become an active place for people our age. We go to these schools rather than travel to Yale. In PowerPoint class, a fifty-three-year-old speechwriter learned to create and show slides from a laptop computer. More and more, her clients have been moving away from the artsy-crafty type of speech and toward the no-frills presentation with tons of slides. The course saved her career. A man in his late forties with two children has been downsized from his communications job at a benefits company in Westchester County, so he enrolled in real estate classes at a local community college. He's outgoing, honest, and eager to learn. When he interviewed at two real estate agencies, they were both excited by his prospects. However, he remains cautious. If a real estate career doesn't work, he's open to other things, and he's willing to go back to school again.

In addition to colleges and other schools, continuing education programs are sometimes given by many corporations. Training programs for employees are also offered by the same companies. A fifty-eight-year-old former security analyst who took two years off from his field and couldn't get back into it decided to try financial planning and enrolled in a class in a nearby company. Many retirees were also in the class. Retirees are the new wave of professionals who go on to a second, third, and even fourth career. *Fortune* profiled them and observed that they seek new career challenges not just for the money but because they love their new pursuit.

TRAINING AT $30 BILLION A YEAR

Learning doesn't always come cheap. A communications freelancer wanted to move into investor relations. Each course she took cost her about $800. The bill for corporate America to train its people each year comes to about $30 billion. But professional training isn't just an American phenomenon. In 1996, the Organization for Economic Cooperation and Development went on record highlighting the importance of lifelong or continuous learning for all nations.[2]

WE'RE ALL ON ASSIGNMENT

There is so much emphasis on continual learning because the global marketplace and the information revolution have raised the standards for what we need to know, and often we have to do our work with less briefing and supervision. That has led to profound change in the work world. Workers, for instance, are fired faster. There isn't time to settle in anymore.

Today, we end up holding many different types of jobs in our careers. The top-drawer speechwriter might be doing work in marketing communications one year and investor relations the next. As *HR Magazine* puts it, "Careers have become a collection of assignments."[3] Gone are the days of predictable employment.

In the past, seven people might have been dedicated to shareholder and employee publications in a particular company and they could count on doing that for years. Now, those communicators would keep getting re-assigned to new projects. To do those new jobs they would have to get up to speed with new skills quickly. During the 1980s, when IBM was first showing signs of trouble, marketing and sales departments sent an invitation to the communicators to join them. Those who opted for the change certainly learned a lot—fast. As the electric utility industry is becoming deregulated and facing competition, there's also a quick change of roles. At one utility the researcher became an expert on competitive intelligence.

"OLD"

In a focus group I conducted with young professionals, they all agreed that the people who came across as "old" in the office were those who refused to learn new things. Those young people are right on the money. "Old" means staying with the status quo. There was a colleague I knew who bragged that he never went to an International Association of Business Communicators seminar, never took a course in new media, never bothered to learn to read a balance sheet. When his consumer products company had a layoff, he went in the first wave.

EARN AND LEARN

The survivors among us know or have found out that to keep earning we've got to keep learning. The new game is all about thinking and acting smart. General Electric's Jack Welch, one of the most successful leaders in corporate America, is considered very smart. He implemented many changes at GE *before* these changes became a trend in corporate America, which gave GE a distinct competitive advantage. Bill Gates, the head of Microsoft, made some self-defeating moves to deal with the antitrust pressure on the company. He isn't considered so smart after all.

Bobbie Prezio from southern New Jersey was laid off from her job at a health care facility. She was sixty-five years old at the time and was determined to keep working. When the unemployment office offered her training in office skills, she was smart and jumped at the opportunity. "Today," says Prezio, "I'm taking business math, accounting, business English, Excel, Microsoft Word, and Power-Point." Prezio is confident about getting a job in a new field because "employers realize that at my age I'm coming to a job to work, not to climb the ladder." Prezio plans to continue taking courses. She'd like to become a paralegal.

Paul Hoffman is now in his forties. Since he has been on his own since he was fifteen, he "got it" right away that he was only as marketable as what was in his head and the skills that he had learned. Right now Hoffman is in the housepainting business. People who know him think of him as smart. He seems to get work no matter what's happening in the marketplace. However, he knows that in five or ten years he'll be too old for this kind of work, so he's preparing for a second career by taking a broad range of courses, including writing, conversational German, judo, and whatever else will keep his mind and body active. He might finish up his college degree and train to be a counselor.

LEARNING ALL THE TIME

In addition to taking courses, attending corporate training programs, and working for degrees, we're also learning informally. From watching shows like *Larry King Live* and analyzing the reactions of the guests we watch how people present themselves when they're under pressure. We're also learning to pick up trends from the street quickly enough to apply that knowledge to our work. (Levi Strauss, incidentally, has assigned a networker to keep tabs on what's going on in the inner city.) We're listening to a lot of stories about people our age who are out of work. From these, we are often able to distill a list of things *not* to do if we want to remain employed.

EFFICIENCY

Not all paths to learning are efficient. A psychotherapist with a master's degree considered going for a Ph.D. because a doctorate would enhance her credentials. She realized, however, that working full time for a doctorate wasn't efficient because it meant she would have to cut back on her practice and, including the cost of opportunities lost, the fee for the degree would total more than $250,000. Instead, she has decided to build her practice by developing a specialization that is in demand.

An ambitious corporate writer took two years off to get an MBA and then returned to writing. That was very inefficient. In addition to the opportunity cost of two years off the job, the MBA hasn't given him increased mobility. He could have acquired much of the same knowledge by trying out a variety of communication fields.

It's usually more efficient to learn while you're employed. An executive in a Hartford-based insurance company always wanted to teach grade school, so he became certified while he was still employed full time. When his job was abolished he was able to easily change careers to teaching.

An investor relations profession in his seventies always dreamed of having his own shop. While he was still employed, he talked with over one hundred self-employed people and found out what was needed to start up a business, what the hours were like, what they did in slow times, and how they managed to meet a payroll. He concluded that he would rather remain a "working stiff" and forgot about being an entrepreneur.

A speechwriter knew he was tired of writing speeches and was considering getting out of public relations entirely. He volunteered for an interdisciplinary task force to find out what else was available in the company. Eventually he decided to stay in public relations, but he didn't miss a beat in his career.

Smart learners learn from other people's experience and from within the company.

THE LEARNING ORGANIZATION

Back in 1990, Massachusetts Institute of Technology professor Peter Senge predicted in *The Fifth Discipline: The Art and Practice of the Learning Organization* that our learning would be continuous.[4] There would no longer be boundaries between college and the real world, or graduate school and a profession. Whether on our jobs or in our own business, on or off duty, we would still be learning new things.

Additional learning gives us a competitive advantage. A forty-three-year-old computer specialist was laid off from a financial services company. The first thing he did was sign up for evening courses, and within five months he obtained a lucrative consulting contract.

Continuous learning, says the *National Underwriter*, a leading insurance industry trade magazine, is part of the new concept of how work is done. The notion of only being "on duty" between nine and five is gone.[5] In my business, clients no longer apologize if they request you do something after hours. For example, one client expected the account team to watch the last episode of *Seinfeld* in case some material from it could be used in his speech. You can bet they did it.

NOT JUST I.Q.

When I was in high school, a lot of fanfare was made about the students who had the highest I.Q.s. They went on to be finalists in the National Merit Scholarship Program and made all us "normal brights" look pretty bad. But few of those high-I.Q. folks made it big. Scientist Howard Gardner told us why. In his breakthrough book, *Frames of Mind: The Theory of Multiple Intelligences*, he pointed out that there is more to intelligence—and success—than I.Q. Gardner said that there were seven types of intelligence:

- Verbal intelligence. Why does Ted Koppel handle himself on his show so well while Jesse Jackson doesn't? It's verbal I.Q. Some of us present ourselves better than others. We can do that in person, on paper, or on the Internet. Despite his stutter, General Electric's head Jack Welch is verbally highly intelligent because he presents himself so well.
- Musical intelligence. Elvis and the Beatles knew how to create

new sounds that would get the attention of the world. John Williams has made films more memorable by composing just the right score. Smart events planners buy the rights to use certain music for their occasions.

- Logical intelligence. These people see cause and effect or the lack of cause and effect when everyone else accepts conventional wisdom. They're the iconoclastic thinkers, like management consultant Peter Drucker.

- Spatial intelligence. It was this kind of intelligence that helped Frank Lloyd Wright create a new kind of architecture. People who are intelligent in this way are the ones who converted Manhattan factory floors and warehouses into co-ops.

- Bodily intelligence. We've all seen how Michael Jordan can make a basket and Michael Jackson can take over a stage. Princess Diana knew the exact body language to use to come across as regal yet accessible.

- Intrapersonal intelligence. These are the kinds of folks who can look inward and come out with a poem, a novel, or a personal solution to their problems. They usually become actors, speech-writers, and psychotherapists.

- Interpersonal intelligence. These people are the ones who know exactly what to say and how to say it. They become congresspeople, computer salespeople—and con artists.[6]

By the time we hit forty we're expected to have developed a number of these forms of intelligence in the workplace. Notice how Apple's Steve Jobs and Microsoft's Bill Gates are becoming more cultured as they mature. If we have gaps in our knowledge bases, we're expected to do something about them. When we're twenty-five we can maybe get away with being socially inept or decorating our office like a college dorm room, but that doesn't fly when we're older. We're supposed to "know better"—and we will be penalized if we don't.

THE NERVOUS MARKETER

A friend asked me to interview a marketer who was about fifty and out of work for about a year. The marketer made a bad impression on me because she lacked certain types of intelligence that we expect in a mature professional. For instance, she was interpersonally inept: She was nervous and let it show. She should have fixed this problem by running around the block before she came in or by taking a Dale Carnegie course. The world is unforgiving of a lack of social skills in a seasoned professional. Her logical intelligence was also off. She spoke about her past job, not about what she was doing currently. She couldn't see that it's logical that I would be more interested in what she can contribute now.

TALENT

Today, the multiple types of intelligence are frequently referred to as talent. When it comes to talent, it's a seller's market. The management consulting firm McKinsey and Company surveyed six thousand managers who were asked what they thought was the most important resource. They answered: talent.[7]

RETRAINING TALENT

Frequently, we think about talent mostly in terms of young people. A talented law school graduate will go off to a law firm and develop into a seasoned pro. The parents in my community are very eager to develop the talent in their children, so they send them to baseball and music camps so their talent can be trained.

Talent also has to be nurtured and updated at all phases of our career. Smart professionals are constantly monitoring their talent to see if the meter is moving toward empty. A talented psychiatrist lost patients because he wasn't trained in the new medications for depression. A talented speechwriter started writing boring presentations because she wasn't aware of what the new media was doing to audience's mind-sets. A talented media representative started missing out on placements because he wasn't keeping up with the subtle changes in newspapers and talk shows.

I have learned to keep my interpersonal skills sharp by occasionally going to a gathering or professional meeting involving an area of interest of mine, but where I know no one. Then, I observe how quickly I can engage the attention of the people in the room.

LOVING LEARNING—THE PROS AND CONS

Mary Jane Genova used her intellectual abilities to get out of poverty in Jersey City, New Jersey. She eventually wound up studying for a Ph.D. in English at the University of Michigan and later at Harvard Law School. On a more practical level, Genova has taken continuing education courses in everything from screenwriting to how to relax. She subscribes to many periodicals and is constantly doing research on-line. For the past twenty years, she has been a business writer. I selected Genova to interview because she clearly understands the pros and the cons of the thirst for knowledge.

* * *

INTERVIEW WITH MARY JANE GENOVA

RD: When is the thirst for knowledge a handicap in a career?

MJG: I can only speak for myself. The thirst for knowledge impeded me when I felt I had to do all kinds of background reading before starting a project. I realized how little I knew about a subject and found ways to get more information. The wise thing would have been to do a little background research, ask some experts some questions, and then start writing.

Focusing on everything you don't know can paralyze you. I realized that I'm a writer, not an expert in quality or performance appraisals. My job is to write.

RD: Do you regret any of your formal education?

MJG: Graduate school at Michigan was a good experience in that I learned how to be analytical. I couldn't be an executive writer without this ability to approach a project in a very strategic manner. Looking back on that experience, I would have learned what I needed by getting a master's degree—and then leaving for a job. Working for a doctoral degree was not that helpful.

At the age of forty-something I decided to make a career change to law. I worked hard studying for the Law School Admissions Test (LSAT) and my scores were good enough to be admitted to Harvard Law. My friends said that I was making a mistake trying to embark on such a major career change in my forties, especially since my writing career was going well. They advised me to attend a local law school, such as Rutgers, where I was also admitted, and see if I wanted to make more of a commitment. At Harvard, I quickly realized that I didn't want to go through the stress of starting all over again in a new field. Moreover, I didn't enjoy studying the law, but was praised in class for my writing ability. So, I returned to my writing career. Lesson learned: take a career change in baby steps. Think carefully before committing to a major academic program.

RD: What's the most recent instruction you've had?

MJG: I attended a free seminar at the local library on how to access the Internet. Lots of training is free, to the point, and convenient.

RD: What kind of courses do you want to take?

MJG: I'd like to become more balanced in my writing, so I'm considering taking a course at the New School in writing fiction or writing comedy. It's easy for my thought process to get stale if I'm just writing about business subjects.

RD: What courses are you tempted to take but sense it wouldn't be a good idea?

MJG: I considered taking classes toward a master's degree in animal behavior at Rutgers. During the past four years I've become very interested in animals, and down the road I might want to open a side business dealing with animal care. But my gut tells me that I can't become too diverse in my interests. It's very demanding to earn a living right now, and if I go off in too many directions my writing business could tank.

RD: What's the best way to keep up in your field?

MJG: Read business magazines, watch cable programs on business, and get catalogues from the Harvard Business Press. Part of me would love to go for a master's degree in business at night, but I don't need all that learning. Also, I can't afford to take that much time away from my business.

RD: Do you think that it helps your thinking to teach a course in your field?

MJG: Teaching courses is great for the résumé, but the satisfaction from the experience depends on the interest of the students. I taught an undergraduate course in public relations that students were taking as an elective, and I didn't sense a lot of in-depth interest.

* * *

CHOOSE CAREFULLY

As Mary Jane Genova pointed out, not all learning opportunities are useful to our work. Some may actually be a handicap. An MBA might know so much about business that he or she would be unable to pull it all together and write it up. Also, it's possible to fly off in too many directions, like the perennial learners who are always up on the latest in technology or political thinking. Absorbing all that new knowledge drains their energy.

AGING IS RELATIVE

There are days, of course, when all of us throw up our hands and claim that we can't learn another new thing. Why can't personal computers still run on DOS, and how come Microsoft has to keep putting out new versions of Windows? But most days we accept the new learning realities of the work world, and most of the time we don't have trouble taking in new material. Chronological age is not a good predictor of how an older professional will function. Aging, researchers are finding, is a highly individual process.[8] Management consultant Peter Drucker is highly productive in his nineties, whereas I know some professionals in their thirties who don't have any fire in the belly.

Trauma, however, can cause aging—at any chronological age. In our careers, a trauma such as a layoff or a promotion that doesn't come through can catch us short and might make us feel old. We might act "old." But we can move away from that black hole. Now there are many courses that can help us regroup after a crisis, and in these courses we can meet new people and find out we're not the only ones who have had a setback.

THE FEAR FACTOR

If you've ever been to a Microsoft Word seminar, you probably noticed that everyone in the course over forty probably looked a little apprehensive, while the younger students were more relaxed. We will most likely feel fear when entering any new situation. That's normal.

Psychotherapist Carol Signore says that once we get past that feeling, most older learners become revitalized. We want to take more courses; we want to try more new things.

ASKING THE RIGHT QUESTIONS

Not all learning is created equal. A writer wanted an overview of accounting but didn't ask the right questions and wound up in a course that covered the nuts and bolts of accounting. She wasted nearly $1,000, a hefty sum since she's self-employed.

It's your responsibility to find out what you're getting for your time and money. It's ideal if you can actually sit in on the course before you sign up for it. Ask to speak to former students. Explain your knowledge and skill needs in detail and find out how the gaps will be bridged by the course.

If you aren't getting something concrete from your learning, you're not going to integrate the new material. Patricia Cruell, McDonald's vice president of training, is quoted in *Meetings and Conventions* stressing that adults will only learn if there's a definite payoff on the job; they don't usually learn for the sake of learning.[9] That means you better think twice before going to New York University for a course in business law unless you know that the knowledge will be immediately useful in your business. My business is too competitive for me to take the time out to take a course such as flower arranging purely for pleasure. In my way of thinking, such a course is justified only if it's going to help me better approach my business situation.

Ask questions about what kinds of results the course has generated. Here you don't necessarily need numbers, which are often inflated. Just find out how some of the students are doing now. It also might be useful to talk with the teachers.

JUMP IN THE DEEP END

Some of my colleagues who've lost jobs tried to prepare for new ones by *reading* about new professions. That's usually a mistake. The best way to learn about a new profession is to jump into the pool at the deep end. A colleague wanted to buy a franchise in frozen desserts.

He didn't read about the business. He got himself a part-time weekend job in a store in the mall which sold frozen desserts. He learned plenty.

If we need to learn about the Internet, then we should get hooked up with the Internet and start surfing. Forget buying a book at the bookstore which talks about trends in the Internet.

After years in real estate a man I knew wanted to become a journalist. He found out what he needed to know about the business by taking an entry-level job at a local paper.

Now You Know...

- Continuous learning is a prerequisite to economic survival.
- We can smell someone who isn't keeping up a mile away.
- Not all paths to knowledge are equally efficient.
- Ask the right questions before taking a course.

7

NETWORKING—BUILDING SOCIAL CAPITAL AFTER FORTY

Networking should be a productive form of relaxation. It should be entertaining. It is not cold-calling, and it should not be such hard work.

—Landy Chase, "Networking," *American Salesman*

What Do I Do?

- I'm networking like crazy and nothing is happening.
- I'm at a disadvantage in networking because I have nothing to trade.
- I'd rather die than network.
- Things are going great for me, yet people still tell me to network.

NETWORKS AND EFFICIENCY

A writer tried for twelve years to get an assignment from a particular consulting firm. She periodically sent direct mail. Every now and then they would ask her to send writing samples and she would, but she never got an assignment. When she was at a luncheon she heard about the need for a speech at that firm. From the people at her table, she got specific information about what the speech should cover and the name of the contact person. She got the assignment.

In-your-face contacts with people can get you direct access to the people you need to reach. Face-to-face is a powerful medium, especially in the information age. The people we are speaking with can see that we don't have green hair and that we know all the right buzz words. They can size us up right on the spot, and decide whether to go further. They can see us talking with Pete Jones, whom they know. They can check out our energy level. As a result, we are bound to get more from a networking session than by sending out one hundred pieces of direct mail.

In networking, it's important to come prepared with your own "headline." Within a handful of words, you have to capture your professional identity. A good networking headline is "I'm a ghostwriter for *Fortune* 100 executives" or "I handle all media for Corporation X." In networking, less is more.

CUSTOMIZED NETWORKING

If you check the Internet, you'll find that there are online networks for just about any group. Newspapers feature lists of very specialized networking groups. There are networks for investor relations representatives, entrepreneurs, and those over forty looking for jobs.

NETWORKING—MORE THAN JUST FOR CONTACTS

Networks aren't just to make contacts anymore. In *Inc.*, Donna Fenn points out that a growing number of women business owners are finding capital through networks.[1] Also, networks often function as support groups in a time of career shock. In a recent issue of *Supervision*, Robert Ramsey observed that isolated people such as middle managers are increasingly turning to networking as a way of getting "encouragement, help, and a sympathetic ear."[2] Parents in my community are anxious about having their children in the "right" networks. In addition, the Internet has made it possible to chat with just about anybody, famous and infamous.

In the *Washington Post*, Steven Ginsberg refers to the network phenomenon as "building social capital" and attributes the flourishing of networking partly to the breakdown of social bonds in professional life, especially in the workplace.³ You and I remember the days when work was a place to make a friend or two. No more. In a world of global competition in which our job might disappear tomorrow, we're all on guard. And in our own businesses, new competition might be a current client—who knows too much about us. Alas, competition among coworkers, for better or worse, has intensified. The old ties, the old ways to cultivate professional relationships, are disappearing. Joe Smith in marketing is more likely to have "friends" in accounting than in his own department. Smith is too aware to trust anyone in his own department.

Networking now provides a relatively "safe" environment in which we can shop around for the things we need, ranging from information and contacts to the warm and fuzzies. And more and more of us are seeking out that environment. I know people who buy the local newspaper or a magazine like *Crain's New York Business* solely for the listings of networking opportunities. Networking places have become the *Cheers* of the professional world.

In my business I have to network extensively. Every year, for example, I travel to Davos, Switzerland, to an economic conference to find out what experts around the world are thinking. When I return, clients, staff, and even the security guards want to hear about any new insights I've picked up. Just about every fall I travel back to my alma mater, Notre Dame, for some of the warm and fuzzies that are harder to come by in professional life. There I learn about what the next generation thinks, and I used some of that material in *The Critical Fourteen Years of Your Professional Life*. I encourage my staff to get out of the office and attend a meeting of the International Association of Business Communicators (IABC) or the Conference Board. Networking has become the new DNA for how business gets done, how reputations are made, who lands on their feet when they're laid off, and who gets financing for their businesses.

DISAPPOINTMENTS

Not all of us are getting as much out of networking as we think we should. In *Networking on the Network*, Phil Agre explains that some of us make a bad impression on-line and are not making the contacts we had hoped for.[4] I know a couple who see themselves as master networkers and are active in an Ivy League club in Manhattan. Both are currently out of work and have been unemployed for a while. Because they're dealing from a position of weakness, they're not getting as much from this networking resource as they could otherwise.

Many of my colleagues wonder why they aren't making the high-level connections they expected to make at certain country clubs. Through the grapevine I've heard that some big-time networkers are being perceived as pests. In this era of caller ID, their calls aren't being taken.

Networking by itself won't get us anything unless we do it right. If we've just lost a job, we should pull ourselves together before we go networking, because people on the network expect that we have something to "trade" in return for their help. If we're in bad shape, we obviously don't have too much to trade.

DIGNITY

Some of us are learning that there are different ways to approach networking when we are over forty than when we were under forty. I bet entrepreneur-turned-corporate-executive Ted Turner conducts himself quite differently at a business conference than does a kid in his first job. Could you imagine Warren Buffett or Elizabeth Dole hurrying to gather up hundreds of business cards at a networking meeting? Also, at our age, selecting with whom to network is key. There are some groups I keep away from because being associated with them can tarnish my reputation. I'm interested in preserving my dignity while I network.

To help sort out how we should approach networking, I've brainstormed with communications consultant Carol Kinsey Goman, Ph.D. Her present consulting practice is her third vocation, and she started it at the age of forty. Her books include *This Isn't the Company I Joined*. Through her firm, Kinsey Consulting Services, in Berkeley, California, Goman helps executives connect effectively with all their constituencies, ranging from employees and shareholders to customers and the government.

* * *

INTERVIEW WITH CAROL KINSEY GOMAN

RD: Since you've started a new career at forty, I know that you have a special interest in the age issue.

CG: Yes, I do. When I started being a consultant at forty, I knew that I would have to sell myself. When you're going to sell yourself, you must take inventory of what you have, what you can offer, and what your deficits are. When I started out I wanted to do consulting work with large organizations, but I hadn't worked in a large organization. I couldn't say that I had worked at IBM for ten years or the U.S. government for five years. What I did have, though, was experience in problems that large organizations at the time were facing. In my second career as a psychotherapist I had dealt with guiding people through change, and corporations were and are going through plenty of change. Here, I was able to position age at an advantage. Because of my age I had plenty of know-how in helping to turn change into an opportunity for growth—of profits, of skills—you name it. A thirty-year-old right out of graduate school or business school couldn't offer what I could.

Another skill I had was the ability to present myself and my material in a way that caught people's attention. In my first career I had been in show business. Therefore, in my new career I could help executives develop a presence and get a message across. Years back, when I was in performing arts, I wouldn't have known how to leverage this experience, but by the age of forty I recognized that most of my previous experience was useful—if I positioned and packaged it right. After forty, our experience really does pay off.

RD: Carol, does the forty-plus person need a different persona or image than those under forty when trying to network?

CG: Absolutely. This goes back to the dignity you talked about, and also to credibility. In the workplace, once you're past forty years of age, it's assumed that you have already proved yourself, otherwise you would be unemployed or would have switched to another career where you could be more successful. A professional identity is supposed to come together by time we get to the big-four-oh.

Therefore, we will confuse people if we sell ourselves as aggressively as we did fifteen years earlier. People will wonder, "If those public relations consultants are selling themselves so much, they must not be 'good' at what they do. Hey, I better watch out." Overselling includes smiling too much, presenting too much paper regarding our credentials, mentioning too many accomplishments, and being too deferential.

Recently I was coaching a female executive who was still selling herself too much. If that behavior had continued, people would start gravitating from her network because they would feel confused: How could such a successful person be pitching herself like a struggling would-be artist out of the Broadway play *Rent?*

After the age of forty we don't sell ourselves, per se. What we do is explain how, through our experience and skills, we can add value to an organization. We have to talk in specific terms, such as "I helped Corporation X with its crisis. Its stock has recovered. I know that I can also help you. Would you like to meet?"

We also have to become more of a visionary. If we're at a meeting of our professional society we should be able to speak about the direction of our field in broad terms. We have to have a feel for what the economy will be like in the next century, and be aware of emerging trends.

As we age, another thing people expect is that we're less obviously competitive. We should be able to work well with others by the time we're forty. At our age we shouldn't be so full of ourselves.

In addition, we expect to see what I call conscious confidence in professionals who are past forty, that is, we should be aware of our strengths, what we're good at. If we don't know what we're good at, then we better take stock. While we network, we have to be keenly aware of what we have to offer. Again, this goes back to taking inventory. Networking, you might say, is one of the oldest forms of bartering.

RD: What message should we be sending when we're on the network?

CG: The number one message we should be sending is that we're credible, and that credibility comes with experience and the conscious confidence I've discussed. Here, we should back away from overselling ourselves and be more relaxed, because we really know our worth and value. At the same time, we have to communicate that we are very open to new experiences. This is a powerful combination: being grounded in our personal credibility while being very open to new avenues of experience.

RD: One big problem many of us over forty have is attracting those under forty to our network. We need to associate with young people to get to know their mind-sets, what they're reading, what they're watching and listening to. My son, Geoffrey, is a key person on my network.

CG: One good way of attracting young people is to offer to mentor them. There are many, many young people who know they need a mentor but have been unable to find one. But not all mentors are created equal. We really have to have a genuine interest in the young person. My father, who died at eighty, had a tremendous rapport with young people. He had the ability to see the talent in a young person, and they knew that he cared about them.

RD: One big challenge in networking is to attract people who can really help you. How do you advise people to attract those with power and influence?

CG: You attract the powerful and influential the same way you attract anyone else. People are mainly interested in what's in it for them—what we can offer them. But more specifically, there are a variety of ways we can gain access to the kinds of people we need for our careers. We can try to get on a nonprofit board, where we can usually meet well-connected people. Another strategy is to analyze the successful people in our groups. We can try to figure out the obstacles they're wrestling with, and then take an inventory of our skills and experience and see if we can help them get past their obstacles. We can say: "I know that you're trying to get new clients and I can help you."

RD: We're hearing quite a bit about equity in networking. Why is equity, or reciprocity, so important?

CG: In networking—or any other relationship in life—we want to get out of it as much as we put in. That's the equity factor. People in your network will begin to feel uncomfortable if you're taking away more from the group than you're putting in. That's why young people in networks usually do a lot of volunteer work for the group, since they can't offer much in the way of wisdom, experience, or connections.

On the other hand, we might sense that we are providing the network with more than we're getting from it. When there's an imbalance like that, we frequently move on to other networks.

Bob, sometimes I worry that I'm taking more from my relationship with you than I'm giving, but obviously it balances out. We've been networking together for some time now.

RD: I know that you've networked a great deal, Carol. Networking has proved very effective for both of us. But some things we do when we network can turn people off. Suppose you're in California and you walk into the so-called Royal Order of Communicators, and most of the members in that group are over forty. Are there characteristics of an over-forty group that might turn you, and others, off?

CG: After we've achieved a lot in our profession, there's a tendency to sometimes take the attitude: Been there, done that. That kind of mind-set indicates that we have nothing to learn, and people with fresh ideas won't gravitate to us.

RD: In some of the groups I network with, there are often jokes about the so-called midlife crisis. Is that something we really do go through in our forties or fifties?

CG: There really is a phenomenon known as the midlife crisis, and it is often happening as young as thirty. Sometimes it never happens. My father never went through it. But if we do go through a crisis of this sort it can be a fabulous experience. It can shake us out of a static situation and we can look at ourselves and our options with new eyes. Often people who are able to make these kinds of breakthroughs in their ways of seeing the world really stand out in networks.

RD: What's the most effective kind of networking?

CG: I know a seventy-year-old woman who networks all the time, including when she does her laundry. Networking is a way of life with her. When her husband needed a kidney transplant, this woman networked and came up with three donors. People like her are relationship focused. They use every social situation as an opportunity to network. They also don't burn bridges.

RD: What are the red flags that your networking efforts aren't going well?

CG: That brings us back to the equity factor. If there is an imbalance of any kind, we're in trouble. We may be contributing too much or not enough.

RD: I've been hearing about "informal networking." What can you say about that?

CG: Actually, all our social interactions are chances to network. Look around the office and you'll notice that some people are always focusing on other people. That's informal networking. Informal networking is when you strike up a conversation on a plane with the person in the next seat or you get to know the person who delivers the mail. I don't formally network. I'm able to accomplish what I need to in terms of contacts through my normal business and social activities. Formal networking usually means going to an association's meeting or sending out letters requesting informational interviews. That works very well for some people. There's no one best method.

* * *

THE ART OF NETWORKING

In short, networking depends a lot on our attitude and how we present ourselves. In the corner of every networking group are some unhappy-looking people who don't want to be there. It shows and they usually don't accomplish much.

In addition, networking is an art. If you want it to work for you, you will keep learning more about how to master all the factors associated with it, and those factors keep changing. When corporate America was fat and happy—and the top dog in the global marketplace—the art of networking was pretty primitive. At a meeting of a networking group, it was okay to go up to Joe Smith, vice president of public relations at General Widget, introduce yourself, and offer some platitude such as that General Widget is a very fine company. No more. Before you go to the meeting, you should be aware of who might be there and do research on those persons and their organizations. From that research you should be able to approach those people in a way that they get something from the encounter—maybe new insight, the name of a useful article to be scanned, the name of someone doing similar work. This process is now part of the investment you've got to make in building social capital in a global marketplace.

One more thing about the art of networking: like all art, networking benefits from genuine creativity, and this doesn't mean just getting the e-mail address of the CEO of Colgate-Palmolive. It means using your imagination to create a message that will get the CEOs attention and lead that person to put you on the organization's radar screen.

But creativity also involves risk. One networker wrote to the CEO of a women's clothing firm. She was critical of the approach and wording of the firm's new promotional material and suggested another approach. The CEO did respond—angrily. That was one relationship that never got off the ground.

Any art also demands planning—lots of it. Orson Welles just didn't gather some people together and decide to make a movie happen. Like all artists, he did strategic planning on how *Citizen Kane* should be made. An important step in planning, says Phillip Agre, is for us to know our goals.[5] Those of us who scan the newspaper and decide to attend a meeting of a particular professional organization will be disappointed if we don't have a clear idea of why we're going. And our goals might change over the months we go to the organization. The goal must be concrete, for example, to get leads on how to look for a job after forty years of age. It can't be vague, such as to connect with people who would contribute to animal rights.

A former financial broker wanted to enter public relations. She attended IABC meetings in hope of learning more about the profession. That goal was too unfocused, so she never got much out of the organization. Since she looked lost there, she also made a poor impression. She would have fared better had her goals been clearer, and included, for instance:

- Learning about the new technological tools in the profession
- Connecting with people who are in a position to hire entry-level professionals
- Getting on a committee dealing with technology, since technical know-how is usually a strength of young people

THE NINE GUIDELINES

For those of us over forty, there are at least nine guidelines for networking.

ENJOY THE PROCESS

We've all encountered the wild-eyed networkers who are intent on meeting everybody in the room—in ten minutes. That's not fun. President Bill Clinton has been called the Network President, and I bet no one has ever seen him visibly dread a social event.

People we encounter while networking represent a gold mine of information, leads, and contacts. Enjoy gaining access to these treasures. If you are a bull in the china shop socially, you might think about getting a coach or signing up for a Dale Carnegie course. You can also study how people good at networking get and hold the attention of other people.

HAVE SOMETHING TO TRADE

Networking is built on reciprocity. I help get your son a job at an ad agency and you help get me access to the CEO of Global Motors so I can have a shot at getting him as a client. Everyone has something to trade, even during unemployment or other career shocks. Before you go out there and network, take stock of what you can offer. Maybe it's advice on how to get a good score on the LSAT; maybe it's names of people to contact at Paine Webber; maybe it's where to get high-quality printing at low rates; maybe it's knowing about a small cottage at the beach that can be rented cheaply for the summer.

The advantage of being over forty is that we have plenty to trade. We have our skills down. We know a large number of people. Many owe us favors. We've proved that we know how to survive many situations. We know about the corporate cultures of a number of organizations, and what the gatekeepers at certain corporations look for in a résumé. We probably can tell useful anecdotes about career changes we've considered.

DIVIDE AND CONQUER

If we know our goals, we will be able to select groups which give us a good return on our time investment. *Inc.* recounts the story of food

entrepreneur Fran Lent. When she started her business, Lent discovered that a new type of resource was emerging—networks created
specifically for entrepreneurial women. Through the Women's Economic Network, she gained access to CEOs in the food industry.[6] A
freelance writer I know heard that the Newark–Jersey City, New
Jersey, area was attracting large organizations relocating from Manhattan. It took her a while to find the right groups for networking, and
the ones she initially contacted were basically concerned with small
businesses. Her specialty was preparing materials for the IBMs and
Morgan Stanleys of the world, and her best approach turned out, not
to be joining organizations, but contacting appropriate people right in
their organizations.

BE PATIENT

Networking is a long-term activity. It is about building relationships, and that takes time. The time to become part of a network is
before we need it. Harvey Mackay's networking book is titled *Dig Your
Well Before You're Thirsty*. Develop a network *before* you wake up in a
cold sweat some night and require immediate reassurance.

Richard Kosmicki, who's been in the workforce a number of years
and heads media relations in our office, is a brilliant networker. Part
of his success is due to his talent in dealing with people. The other
part is due to his persistence. Kosmicki will stick with organizations
and people for decades. He gets to know reporters, editors, and
producers when they first join a newspaper, magazine, or television
station. He'll find out how he can help them. Maybe they need a
source at a consumer products company, or a fast quote from an
expert on intellectual property. When they move on to another job,
Kosmicki stays in touch and asks them about their needs. For him, the
crown jewels are those indispensible personal relationships.

If we anticipate that we'll need guidance with our career in a few
years, we should be on the lookout for the right networking organizations now. Not every one is a good fit. A few people I know checked
out a career support group in Fairfield County, Connecticut, and
complained that the unemployed people in it weren't willing to
consider any job that didn't pay six figures and didn't carry the title of
vice president. I don't advise those who might make a career change

down the road to attend those meetings. The thinking there is too narrow.

Those who try to get fast results from networking too aggressively frequently develop reputations as pests to be avoided. They're the type of networkers, says Chase, who pitch on first meeting and gather tons of cards. Afterwards they will do a call-around and pitch some more.[7]

UNDERSTAND THE CONTEXT

Some people started networking through e-mail before they understood the medium. They would send long messages that would run for several computer screens when emerging e-mail etiquette said to keep a communication short enough for one screen. They would also fail to proofread what they had written, and send several e-mails a day rather than plan one message carefully. As a result, they often irritated those they contacted.

In order to network effectively, we have to understand the useful purpose of each tool. For example, "snail mail" still works well for letters of congratulations, sympathy cards, and birthday cards. Going to the meeting of a trade association might not be the most efficient approach if all we want to do is contact one specific person. It would be better to research that person and send a note showing that we've taken pains to get to know about them. In that note, we could ask for a ten-minute informational interview.

The telephone can still be a good tool, but only if we understand how people feel about phone calls. A vice president at a telecommunications company insists on being contacted by vendors only through fax, e-mail, or snail mail. She will not be interrupted with phone calls.

VOLUNTEER

Most networking organizations have plenty of jobs to get done. Doing these jobs helps you to get to know others in the organization and maybe will teach you a new skill at the same time. When you're over forty, though, you should be careful about what tasks you agree to do. I wouldn't want to be on the committee who puts name tags on guests. For us, the best volunteer efforts involve sharing our extensive expertise. For example, you might offer to speak on how to get a small business through a recession or how to make the transition from middle to senior management.

You can also volunteer on an individual basis. After Mary Jane Genova was downsized out of the former General Foods, she made it a point to help others who later found themselves in a similar situation. Much of her early business as a self-employed freelancer came through those whom she had helped, and when they got new jobs they sent business her way.

ACT, DON'T REACT

Networking calls for plenty of self-control. People are people, and we run into many of them at networking groups. Some will be rude, insensitive, and downright cruel. So what. It never pays to take these monsters on. We will make a bad impression in the group, and the monsters will know that they have hit a tender spot.

When we have suffered a setback or are stalled in our job hunt, for instance, we have to be prepared to reply to our critics without losing our cool. The group will notice that we handled ourselves well, and we will get points for grace under pressure. Several years back, when my career was in limbo, I role-played various responses that I would make to those who hassled me. I tried out those responses on a friend, who helped me to not sound defensive and to avoid self-pity.

KEEP UP

It always looks bad when you say or do something that shows you're out of touch. It's the kiss of death for the over-forty set. There really have been people over forty at network meetings who didn't know *Seinfeld* was over or what *Wired* was. People take the time to come to groups to get information. If they notice that your information is out of date you'll be shunned. Before going to a meeting, scan the headlines on-line.

DON'T IGNORE ALL THE VARIOUS GRAPEVINES

Grapevines are a terrific source of information and contacts. They really are one form of network.

Back before there was a global marketplace, it was considered bad form to be associated with a grapevine. Gossip was verboten. In the late 1970s, a middle manager at the former Gulf Oil was severely reprimanded for disseminating gossip. Now, even the *Harvard Business Review* publishes articles on how to gain access to the grapevine.[8] The landmark book *Corporate Cultures* carries a chapter on grapevines,[9] and people are studying books such as *Emotional Intelligence* to improve their ability to gain access to grapevines.[10]

I've found that the most effective approach to the grapevine is to have multiple identities. The managers of accounting who just sit in their offices aren't going to get much information or form too many relationships outside the department. You've got to widen your sphere of influence. Smart managers find reasons to go to other parts of the organization, and when they're there often enough, they get information. Smart managers are also in the habit of sending e-mail all over the organization.

Another good strategy is to always have gossip to share. That means you must scout around before you want some particular bit of gossip, picking up interesting tidbits about other issues. But we don't want to share our own store of gossip too freely. That lessens our negotiating power and can get us labeled as a bigmouth.

A WAY OF LIFE

In the new economy, networking has to become a way of life. I never miss the chance to network with anyone, including my sons' friends and the contractor who installed our pool. My wife, Jan, is thrilled when she makes a new contact. Then why aren't all of us over forty taking advantage of this great tool called networking? There can be an undertow of isolationism as we age. Some gerontologists state that with age comes a look inward: We become less concerned with the external world and more concerned with ourselves.[11] I'm convinced that's very individual. We *never* have to lose our focus on the world. Turning inward *doesn't* have to happen. If we migrate toward people we're comfortable with, we can remain engaged in the world, relationship focused rather than self-focused. That's why we should carefully choose where and with whom we want to network.

Now You Know...

- Networking in itself doesn't guarantee results. We have to know what we're doing.
- We have to approach networking differently after forty.
- The bottom line on networking is: "What's in it for me?"
- We can improve our networking skills.
- Networkers keep focused on the outside world, not themselves.

8

IF IT'S A JOB YOU WANT

Junk the outdated myths of one job, one career, and one loyalty, and replace it with focus on your *survival, rather than that of the corporation.*

—Martin Yate, *Beat the Odds*

What Do I Do?

- I have two kids in college. I can't fool around with temporary work. I need a job.
- I get interviews for full-time jobs but no offers.
- Jobs are all I know.
- I have a job offer but I don't want to take it.

JOBS AFTER FORTY

Why do some professionals have trouble getting full-time jobs after forty while others always seem to land on their feet? A man I went to college with has been between jobs more than he's been working. Why? One of my neighbors, on the other hand, got laid off from an aerospace company and very quickly found a *better* job at a specialty-chemical firm. People told him that it's hard to get a job after working in aerospace, but he sailed through the whole process.

This difference in success in finding full-time jobs as we age is a serious issue to ourselves, our families, and society. According to the

U.S. Bureau of Labor Statistics, 14.2 percent of the workforce will be over 55 by the year 2005.[1]

JOBS ARE WHAT YOU KNOW

We're hearing a lot about becoming entrepreneurs, free agents, and various sorts of consultants, but the reality, observes human resources expert Martin Yate, is that the five generations of professionals in America have been conditioned to go to jobs.[2] They *like* jobs. They want to be associated with brand-name corporations. They know how to manage the boss, deal with coworkers, and work the grapevine. To get and keep a job, they have been always ready to make major sacrifices. They're willing to relocate or learn a new industry. They're willing to put in long hours.

WHO GETS JOBS?

Professionals who like full-time jobs are moving mountains to find them. And they *are* finding them. According to Steve Harrison, president of the career transition search firm Lee Hecht Harrison, there are a number of key variables that determine who get jobs—no matter what their age—and who have to take other routes to make a living. I recently spoke with Harrison about this issue, and he provided some fresh insights.

THE PERSPECTIVE FROM A CAREER TRANSITION FIRM

Steve Harrison has been with Lee Hecht Harrison (LHH) since 1982. He's passionate about keeping people employable. Harrison is an officer of Adecco, formerly Adia Personnel Services, and serves as chairman of the board of LHH's U.K. operation. He's on the board of directors of Jobs for America's Graduates, the nation's largest and most successful school-to-work program. He is also a charter fellow of the International Board of Career Management Certification. Before joining Lee Hecht Harrison, he was a partner with the Center for Diagnostic Medicine in New York, which provides executive and occupational health services. Prior to that, Harrison spent fourteen years at Tenneco, specializing in labor relations and human resources.

* * *

INTERVIEW WITH STEVE HARRISON—THE BIG PICTURE

RD: The sixty-four million dollar question today is why do some people over forty seem to get jobs so effortlessly while some never get another full-time job after they're laid off?

SH: There are a number of interrelated factors. One is the industry. Some industries can seem predisposed toward younger talent. If you're part of that kind of industry—say, entertainment—you know that your career may be short, and have to plan for that. On the other hand, there are industries that are age neutral. They include academia, manufacturing, health care, law, financial planning, and so on—even the outplacement industry! In some of these, age may even be a plus.

The level of job being sought is another factor in who gets jobs. If the job is in the senior levels of the firm, your age could be a plus. If it's at the manager or mid-staff level, then your age could work against you. Once again, this consideration tends to be industry or role specific.

A third factor is your age itself. I don't see much trouble with those in their forties who are looking for work. The difficulty might start in the fifties, but, as I said, not necessarily. In fact, I'm seeing somewhat less bias about age overall.

A fourth factor is how strategically you've approached your career. I advise my clients and even my children to always think in strategic terms when they make choices about what to do professionally, or what not to do. For instance, rather than being a camp counselor during the summer, my son or daughter would be wiser to get an internship at a company. The latter experience will be more useful to his or her career and more impressive on a résumé. Careers must be carefully planned; they can't just happen. Its every aspect has to help your employability. Would it help your credentials if you had experience in global marketing? You bet. Then it's your responsibility to get the experience you need.

A fifth factor is how well you've taken care of yourself. I mean everything from physical fitness to how you handle any bitterness about getting laid off. I predict that if you haven't been taking care of yourself you're going to hurt your chances in the interview. Something like your language may reveal that you have a chip on your shoulder.

RD: If I could sum up what you've said, then is it fair to say that your overall message is that each of us has to take responsibility for keeping ourselves employable, from how we look to what skills we can offer in the marketplace?

SH: That's right. But this is also a national issue. The fastest-growing age group is those between thirty-five and fifty-five. One part of that issue is that there's a skills shortage in certain fields, such as technology. National policies have to create a match between what we have to offer and the skills in demand.

RD: Say someone our age just lost a job in high tech or financial services. What should he or she do?

SH: First of all, he has to admit to himself that some, not all, employers see us as "less than." For instance, some employers may assume that we can't keep current in technology—that's a given that we have to accept.

Second, the newly unemployed should take a long walk on the beach, and a wholistic approach in seeing themselves. They should ask, "Am I contemporary? Have I kept up my appearance? Have I been reading the latest business thinking? Have I been keeping current with contemporary issues such as globalization? What are my strengths? How can I highlight my strengths to an employer?"

We also have to realize that it's in our employer's self-interest to try to retain us once we're hired. That's a plus. Employee retention is now a national concern. It is expensive to keep refilling positions. Leadership is another important area where we have to evaluate ourselves. It's a downsized world. There are fewer chiefs. That means that we all have to pitch in and help lead. When hiring, employers are looking for executives who can lead immediately. I suggest that candidates read up on leadership or take a seminar.

RD: Is there anything else the newly unemployed should do?

SH: They have to get the mind-set that the next job may be temporary, in that it may only last three to five years. So we're all getting ready for the *next* job, which means that even when we have a job we should be reading Hal Lancaster's column in the *Wall Street Journal* and keeping up our network. It's fatal to start building a network the day we lose a job. The time to network is when everything is going well, because networking gives us immediate access to the hidden job market.

RD: How does someone prevent himself or herself from seeming "out of touch" in job interviews?

SH: Employers want employees who are "with it." They want employees who can turn on a dime, have the endurance to put in long hours when necessary, and understand what skills they have to offer. Here, employees might have to do some self-assessment. Usually, by our age, it's necessary to "unbundle" our skills and emphasize those which are of use to employers. If someone in public affairs unbundles his or her skills, they might find that they can also work in human resources or marketing. Job descriptions are changing radically. What was once needed in public affairs may not be marketable any more. Unbundle. This won't be too difficult if employees have peripheral vision about what the workplace needs.

We can also present ourselves as valuable if we can influence behavior in the workplace without the title or the authority that bosses once had to own. Titles mean less today. What counts is performance and leadership. Those are the value drivers. We should be able to influence and get results without being the vice president of finance.

RD: What are the common mistakes job seekers make when they hunt for new positions?

SH: The most common is to harbor a resentment about a layoff. Resentments come in all sorts of ways, particularly body language. We have to see losing a job as a normal happening in a new, more competitive global economy.

In interviews, it's also a mistake to be focused only on talking about the job. That kind of one-dimensional intensity frequently means that the person may be a candidate for early burnout. It is better to also have other interests to discuss. Demonstrate that you know how to recharge your batteries through your hobbies.

Before the layoff, have a plan B already in mind; that'll prevent desperation. While working at the job, pick up a real estate license or new skills writing for cyberspace. People who know that they can make a living in a variety of ways interview better.

RD: If you could give only one message to older workers, what would it be?

SH: Keep current. Take care of yourself. No one else will.

* * *

THE NUTS AND BOLTS OF JOB HUNTING

There is now so much advice on how to get jobs that it's easy to become confused. Trying to follow all that advice could make you come across as a "professional job seeker" who has become expert at looking for jobs but who excels at nothing else.

PETER—PROFESSIONAL JOB HUNTER

One of these professional job seekers was a colleague I'll call Peter. Peter was out of work for about two years. He knew exactly how long after a job ad appeared that he should answer it. He was a regular in networking circles such as the IABC. He had a "lucky" suit he wore to job interviews. He knew exactly how to handle the salary question and the one about what he had been doing the past two years. He got so engrossed in the mechanics of getting a job that he never got one. He basically presented himself as a job-hunt robot.

STAN—OTHER IRONS IN THE FIRE

On the other hand, there was a colleague I'll call Stan. When his company was taken over and he lost his job as vice president, he immediately went out and signed up with three or four temporary agencies. It was tough for him to juggle his schedule to go to interviews for full-time jobs when he was working temp jobs, but he knew that if he didn't continue working in some form he would lose his confidence. Stan also went to the community college at night and took courses on how to write for publication. He looked into training to be a chef. The message he gave potential employers was: my time is valuable. Within eight months after the layoff, Stan got a better job than the one he had lost.

BALANCE

There's a cliché that the only way to find a job is to make looking for one a full-time pursuit. Not necessarily. Those who look for jobs full time easily lose perspective on who they are and what they're offering the work world.

TALK WITH FRIENDS WHO ARE WORKING

The most efficient way to prepare for a job hunt is to talk with friends your age who are still working. They're doing something right. Here is how they can help you.

YOUR RÉSUMÉ

Ask to see your friends' résumés. Study the format of several and from them, create an approach to your own. There is no one way to do a résumé. The bookstores are full of models. Amazon.com, the electronic bookstore, lists 443 books on résumés. Take a look at different models to give you confidence in your approach.

CANDID FEEDBACK

When your résumé is done, ask for candid feedback from friends and executive search firms. But it's your call if you want to follow their advice. Incidentally, a résumé is a work in progress. As you gain new insights about how you're presenting yourself or develop new skills or accomplishments, revise your résumé.

SCANNABLE RÉSUMÉS

You're bound to run into companies that make the first cut on résumés by scanning them, or putting them through a computer. If the résumé doesn't have certain keywords such as *Internet experience* or *Microsoft Word*, it'll be knocked out of the box. It's your responsibility to know the keywords in your field.

YOUR AGE

Should you include dates like graduation from college, which give away your age? I've found that if employers are biased against the older worker, it won't help to put off the inevitable when they actually meet you and discover your age. So be up-front about it.

UNBUNDLING

Harrison suggested that we unbundle our skills. That's right on the money. A colleague did a public affairs résumé and a human-resources communications résumé. She had two sets of skills, and it would confuse an employer if she included both in one résumé. Another colleague did one résumé that highlighted his skills in speech-writing and another that emphasized his skills in media placement.

When you sort out your skills, if your discover that you have five sets, then you should do five résumés.

ACCOMPLISHMENTS

Most résumés lack a section for accomplishments. Yours should indicate that you've cut departmental costs in two years by 43 percent, or after you took over the newsletter, surveys showed that readership went up 63 percent, or you created an executive communications department for the company.

THE COVER LETTER

Ask friends what kinds of cover letters get their attention. The purpose of the cover letter is to break through the clutter of applications that come in and get the reader to go to the next step and look over yours.

I've found that job candidates have to try out a number of cover letters before they hit a home run. A strong cover letter is short—no more than one page. It contains experience, skills, and accomplishments, bundled in such a way to make the candidate a good fit for the job, the company, and the industry. That means that you have to do research in the library or on-line. If you find that the company you're applying to is in the midst of a turnaround, then you would highlight your results in turnarounds.

Common pitfalls with cover letters are:

- Too general. Not customized to the particular position.
- Do not deliver a core message, such as "I get results, even under adverse conditions."
- Present a collection of facts rather than integrate the facts into a smooth narrative.
- Do not lead the reader to see what's in it for him or her if they hire the person.
- Do not contain keywords such as *technological background* or *results*.

WHERE TO GET JOB LEADS

In the 1999 edition of *What Color Is Your Parachute? A Practical Manual for Job-Hunters and Career-Changers*, Richard Bolles points out that most jobs aren't advertised. You hear about this hidden job market by writing to companies, networking,[3] and contacting executive search firms.

UNSOLICITED RÉSUMÉS

One job-finding strategy is to send unsolicited letters to those companies you'd like to work for. If you want a mid-level job, you would send your letter to the vice president of the appropriate department. If you want a more prestigious job, you might contact the CEO. There's a payoff in all this work. Frequently, the letters are a way of making contact with someone inside the organization. You might be invited to come meet with the insiders. If you're lucky, there may be an actual position available or one that will soon be.

This way of targeting is especially useful if you want to work in a certain industry or geographical location.

NETWORKING

If you get out there and talk with people from other companies, you may find out that a position is opening up. You may also find out from the horse's mouth what kind of person they're looking to fill it. Networking, unlike answering blind ads, tells you a lot about the real specifications a job entails.

The trick about networking is that it can't be used as an emergency device. You have to build your image in the network long before you'll ever need help. If you're busy at your job, the last thing you want to do is break away and attend a luncheon meeting of some business association. Well, you'll have to make the time for this. You'll also have to invite other contacts to lunch or to see a Yankees game. Socializing makes the new economy function smoothly.

EXECUTIVE SEARCH FIRMS

Some companies have long-term relationships with executive search firms that know the company's corporate culture and only present suitable candidates. Frequently, the heads of executive search firms will have on-going relationships with the company's CEO and be treated as a confidant.

As with networking, the time to introduce yourself to the staff of an executive search firm is when things are going great for you, because the image of strength you present will stick in their minds. Smart professionals keep in touch with these firms about twice a year, keeping them informed of any new developments in their careers. Also, once they're hired, professionals often use the executive search firm that placed them when they have to fill positions. In this way, the bank of favors is built up. When it's time to let an incumbent go, the company will often turn to the search firm to help the dismissed employee find another job.

HELP WANTED

The Sunday newspaper, the Internet, the unemployment office, and support groups frequently carry help wanted ads. Usually, answering these ads is a long shot. Probably hundreds, or even thousands, of others are replying to the same ad. None of those answering have any way of knowing what in their cover letters or résumés will get their applications bounced into the trash pile. Who knows, your salary history may be too much for their blood, or they may have no intention of relocating candidates from east of the Mississippi to Denver, Colorado. But some good jobs do get advertised. Maybe the company doesn't want to pay the fee to an executive search firm, so they are conducting the search themselves. Maybe they had bad luck with the last hire that came through executive search.

If you do get an interview, it's imperative to do your homework to learn what the company is really about. The way to start investigating is to call your contacts and see what they know about the organization and also if they have names of people there you can contact. Research the literature about the company. Many libraries have business reference books that will give you basic facts about a company. Annual reports can be very helpful if it's a publicly traded firm. While you're in the library, check out articles in the financial press about the company. Much of this information is also available online. Your financial planner or broker can also tell you what Wall Street thinks about the firm.

One writer didn't do his homework. If he had, he would have found out that the head of the department he ended up working for was a monster who tormented his staff. He would also have found out that Wall Street considered the company third tier. Within a few months, this writer quit. He could have saved himself a lot of time and aggravation if he knew about these circumstances before he took the job.

THE NONPROFIT ARENA

In the early 1990s, management visionary Peter Drucker brought to the nation's attention that nonprofits were the new model in management. He pointed out that these companies had a deep sense of mission that they combined with sophisticated management tools. "The Girl Scouts, the Red Cross, the pastoral churches," observed Drucker, "our nonprofit organizations are becoming America's management leaders."[4]

Those with the know-how about sophisticated management are being aggressively recruited by nonprofit organizations. In many nonprofits, the compensation has improved. The Internet contains many databases providing nonprofit jobs listings. For example, the Philanthropy Journal (http://www.mncn.org/jobs/) lists jobs available around the country. There are also regional databases, such as the New England Nonprofit Organization Classified (http://www.opnocs.org).

From my work on the board of directors of a nonprofit organization, I've come to admire the resourcefulness of those in the nonprofit
sector. Although they have fewer resources they accomplish more
than the average business. The American Society for the Prevention
of Cruelty to Animals came out with a credit card that funnels a
percentage of your purchases back into the organization. Nonprofits
also learn how to make maximum use of volunteers, and they're
geniuses at getting free publicity.

If I were searching for a job right now, I'd first look into
opportunities with nonprofit organizations to check out how we can
be mutually useful. In a world in which many of us have become
redundant or expendable, it's wonderful to feel needed.

GETTING COUNSELING

Often our best friends are our best professional coaches. They can tell
us when we're coming across as angry and when our confidence has
taken a big hit. But often during a job search we wear out our
friends—and our welcome. We'll constantly replay an interview or
beat them over the head with our unrealistic job hopes for a certain ad
we've answered.

When it's time to give our friends a rest, there are all kinds of other
outlets for help. Where I live, some churches have gotten into the
business of counseling those who are out of work. The cost is usually
low. There are also mental health agencies that help the whole family
get through the ordeal, and many of them charge on a sliding scale.
Chat rooms on the Internet are free. There are also career counselors
whose names you can get from outplacement firms and human
resources departments. There are also weekends of prayer and
meditation. I've heard great things from those who've spent a
weekend at a monastery.

WHEN YOU GET AN INTERVIEW

It's encouraging to get interviews. That means that your résumé and
cover letter are getting results—but you're a long way from home
base. An interview serves as a mutual screening tool. You check out
the corporate culture of the company and see if this is where you want

to be for the next few years. The company, in turn, checks out various aspects of the professional you're presenting to them.

For some companies, the primary objective in interviewing you is to find out if you'll be a good fit for the corporate culture. One old-line computer company was very direct about this with a job candidate. They told her that she wouldn't fit in well at the company, but would probably get a great job somewhere else.

Because so many companies have different agendas when interviewing, it's imperative to find out more about the company before you go for an interview. Some companies test your "band width," or intellectual horsepower, while others are checking to see if you can function without a lot of supervision.

Security analysts can tell you what kind of people a company recruits. Watch *Moneyline* and you'll also get a feel for the corporate culture. Online, there are thousands of articles about companies. The big question is not if they will want you, it's do *you* want to join *them?*

More often than not, it's you who don't like them. You come to Company X and find it's not your style. It's too quiet. The people are impeccably dressed. The human resources person speaks only corporate jargon. The person you would be reporting to is a bully. You would be doing the kind of work that you did fifteen years ago. And they obviously demand a lot of "face time." But the pay and benefits package are really terrific. What do you do? In this case, says psychologist Gary Klein, follow your instincts. Klein contends that we make more decisions than we realize based on intuition.[5]

Suppose we like what we see? How do we make the best impression on an interviewer? Tip number one is the old Erving Goffman advice: Let the person with the most power dictate the terms and conditions of the interview. Follow that lead.[6] The best interviews proceed as a dance, with the person being interviewed knowing exactly the steps to take. If the interviewer asks the candidate about her experience with crisis, the candidate will answer the question succinctly, but will get in all the specifics about her experience and the results she obtained. She was prepared to answer this question because her research about the company showed her that a crisis was looming.

Interviews are opportunities for candidates to pitch their strengths and track records—but only within the parameters set by the interviewer. The interviewer might want to hear only one example of your expertise per question asked. If you go on longer, the odds are you will alienate the interviewer.

With the economy so volatile, most of us are coming to interviews with problems in our past. We have to be ready to answer why we lost a job and what we learned from that. We have to explain why we think we were passed over for a promotion and what we learned from that. We might have to discuss why we stayed at the same company for thirty years and what we learned from that.

We have no control over whether companies will hold the past against us, but at least we can tell our side of the story and convey the wisdom we gained from the experience.

SHOW ME THE MONEY

Many older job seekers move from big companies to smaller ones. That could mean less salary, but it could also mean stock options and pay-for-performance bonuses. If you're starting at a low base pay, you have to realize that it could take a long time to work up to what you used to earn. If you can't handle this, become an entrepreneur or a free agent. Jobs are no longer for you. A fifty-year-old writer took a $10,000 pay cut to get a job, but it ate at her. She wasn't happy at the new job, and it showed.

Money is tricky business. Know how you really feel about it.

HERB BROWN—THE NUTS AND BOLTS

Herb Brown looked for employment twice when he was past forty, and now he hires older workers. He feels passionately that what divides successful job hunters from unsuccessful ones is attitude. Brown has observed, "If you have a positive attitude about going out there and selling yourself and positioning yourself in the marketplace, you've got the lion's share of the battle won already."

Brown is currently chairman and chief executive officer of the Alexander Doll Company, which manufactures collectible and play dolls. He was brought in to turn the company around and in one year he improved profits by a one-third and achieved a 24 percent growth in sales. Before taking the helm at Alexander Doll, Brown was a senior executive at Johnson and Johnson Medical, Inc., Danaher Corporation, Colt Industries, Cummins Engine, and Black and Decker. He is convinced that his performance has been enhanced by the experience gained from working for several major corporations.

* * *

INTERVIEW WITH HERB BROWN

RD: You've been through a number of turnaround situations, and plenty of turnarounds are now happening in organizations. What do older workers offer during a turnaround?

HB: In a turnaround you frequently have to change the organizational culture, and older workers usually have experience with changing cultures. They know how to handle the personal aspects of the changes, and are more sophisticated about the human element. They also have more composure under fire. I got payback on these workers very quickly.

RD: You've looked for a job after forty twice. How did you prepare yourself for that?

HB: The first thing I did was a mind-set thing. I didn't enter the job market with the idea that my age could be an obstacle. I didn't think about who was younger than I and competing for the same job. I kept focused on the skills I was offering, and that kept me on tracks.

I also did some research. I read *What Color Is Your Parachute?* and *Rites of Passage at $100,000.* These gave me good insights on how to present myself in the marketplace, where I had an advantage because I had engaged in job searches in the past.

Next, I put together the support materials I needed. There was the résumé, of course, but there were also financial statements which clearly demonstrated how I had improved the bottom line. I could show quarter-to-quarter movement.

Next, I put together a network of people who could help me. I told them that I was looking for a new opportunity, and they were there for me.

To prepare myself for the new marketplace, I assessed my skills and determined if I should be taking any courses. Today, employers don't want to hear that we can "learn quickly." They want us to already have the skill, to have the initiative to get the skill before we go to them.

My next step in preparing myself for a job search was deciding how I was going to "package" Herb Brown. I did this in a concrete way: I anticipated the questions they would ask me; I prepared talking points about each issue; I kept these points short— anywhere from thirty seconds to two minutes for each one. I also mentally prepared myself for any rejection. In selling yourself, you're not always successful. I knew that I had to be ready for rejection.

Additionally, I had to think through how ˙ .uch "image" I wanted to develop. It's my conviction that we ca. fail if we spend too much time trying to put forth a certain persona. Few of us are actors, and we simply can't pull this off. If you do pull it off, then every day on the job you have to act like the person you presented.

RD: How do you counter the idea that older workers are out-of-date?

HB: It's our responsibility to demonstrate to the company that we're not. This means that our terminology shouldn't be out-of-date. We have to be current with all the new language in our profession. For example, I don't talk about "inventory," I talk about "materials requirement." We also have to clearly demonstrate that we have applied contemporary business concepts to our recent work.

Appearance is also key. We have to look like we take good care of ourselves.

In the actual conversation, we can't wander off on tangents. Stick to the subject matter. Talk in terms of recent accomplishments, the last three to five years. No one wants to hear the war stories from twenty years ago. Volunteer information about your physical activities, such as playing tennis. That shows you're active—and balanced.

Don't let yourself get knocked out of the box on the pay issue. It's assumed that older workers are too expensive for most organizations. You can turn this around by suggesting that more of your compensation is tied directly to performance. That puts you at a lower base, but also gives you opportunity on the bonus side. It also helps reassure the company that if hired, you are willing to make a commitment on your results, that you can commit to improve earnings by a targeted percentage within an established time period.

RD: There is a lot of debate regarding how to do a résumé. Do you have any advice?

HB: I'm a firm believer in the tailored résumé—one that is geared to a specific opportunity. Put yourself in the shoes of the person reviewing the résumé. You want to make it crystal clear that you're the person for the job, and you can do that by tailoring your résumé.

Also, a résumé should tell a story. If you've bounced around from job to job, you want to piece together your experience in a way that creates a smooth narrative. Show continuity where you can.

I disagree with you, Bob, about putting down your college graduation date and other numbers that indicate your age. Why disqualify yourself at the front end? Your goal should be to get in there and be able to sell yourself.

RD: What about attending one of those career support groups?

HB: That all depends on what a particular support group is offering you and what you need. You can usually get a good sense of the group by noticing who's in it. In addition to support groups, there is one-on-one counseling, which can also be helpful. But before you sign any contracts, go to one meeting and see what you get out of it.

RD: What advice would you give to someone who was in the job market for about a year and hasn't received one offer?

HB: I would advise that person to check all his systems, from his appearance to the follow-up after the interview. Obviously, something is wrong. The formula isn't working. At that juncture some soul-searching is in order.

* * *

IT TAKES ONLY *ONE* JOB

When searching for a job, remind yourself that all you need is *one* job. Actually, all most of us can handle at a time is one job. It's irrelevant how many jobs you weren't offered. All that counts is that you did get *one* job, and it's up to you to hold onto it.

Now You Know...

- Jobs may be a little harder to get after a certain age, but people our age do get jobs.
- When we're older there's more to consider in accepting a job offer. For example, can we handle lower compensation or are we willing to try the nonprofit sector? A job may no longer be an option for us. Perhaps we should become entrepreneurs or free agents.
- There are many different ways to approach looking for a job. What counts is what works for us.
- No job is forever. Most only last four or five years. Be ready to start searching for your next job.

9

BEING SELF-EMPLOYED

In 1997, Toby Lenk created what he considered a better way to sell toys—eToys.com. Lenk built his new company on the model of Amazon.com. To pursue this dream, Lenk left his job at the Walt Disney Company.

—Joshua Macht, "Toy Seller Plays Internet Hardball"

What Do I Do?

- My company is having layoffs. I don't think that at my age I can get a comparable job.
- Our company has been taken over by the MBA mentality. I'd like to do work where I can use my own business instincts.
- Work no longer excites me. I'm on Prozac just to cope. Maybe I should start my own business.
- I have some ideas for a small business.

LOOKING AT THINGS DIFFERENTLY

An acquaintance of mine who is my age and handled real estate for a telecommunications company sensed that he would get laid off in a downsizing. He was right. When the axe fell, this former executive roamed the streets of Manhattan, wondering what he was going to do. He walked from 42nd Street to Spanish Harlem. What he noticed was that on every street corner there was a newsstand—owned by immigrants. The streets were lined with food stores and restaurants—owned by immigrants. There were dry cleaners and real estate agencies—owned by immigrants. It dawned on this former executive that he and immigrants had a lot in common: both would find it hard to get good jobs; both knew how to work hard; both wanted control over what they did. This man decided to become an entrepreneur. That was in 1994. Today, he owns four fast-food franchises and would never go back to a corporate position, even if he was made CEO.

Today, because of the new economy and because of our age, our options may be different than they were for the previous generation. We may not be able to stay in our jobs until we retire at around sixty-five years of age. If we lose a "good" job we may not be able to find another "good" job.

Those of us who assumed that we just weren't the "entrepreneurial type" might now consider running our own business. The money seems to be there. A survey by *American Demographics* magazine found that the entrepreneurs interviewed had a median net worth of $3.7 million versus $700,000 for corporate executives.[1] Also, the proliferation of franchises has made it easier to jump in.

SCARY STUFF

For most of us who have been in traditional organizations, going out on our own looks pretty scary. In fact, every time the economy gets better, many of us who thought about starting a business reverse that thinking and go after a job. And some of us who were running a business during a downturn try to get back into a job if the economy recovers. According to the research firm Challenger, Gray, and Christmas, Inc., after the stock market crash of 1987, about 20 percent of downsized workers became entrepreneurs. The economy was bad then, but when it picked up, only 5 percent of displaced workers decided to become entrepreneurs.[2]

On the other hand, according to Steven Bursten in *The Bootstrap Entrepreneur*, two-thirds of entrepreneurs are under the age of forty.[3] In short, becoming an entrepreneur doesn't come easily to us who are over forty.

SUCCESS EQUALS LARGE "BRAND-NAME" ORGANIZATION

Becoming an entrepreneur isn't a natural reflex for many of us over forty because we were conditioned to think that success meant climbing the ladder in a large, prestigious organization. After college or professional school, we headed to the biggies, and life immediately became easy for us. At parties, when we said we worked at IBM or General Motors, everyone knew what we were about. Once we learned to play the game of corporate politics, we could maneuver ourselves out of dead-end jobs in the organization and into positions that were better platforms for getting ahead. The worst that would happen is that we would plateau at fifty and realize that we would never become the president or CEO. I worked in a large organization for decades and it was a good life.

Some of us still have access to that good life. The profile of such figures is this: they are usually low-key, quick studies in new concepts, can take on protective coloring quickly as regimes change, and know how to make their superiors look good. Occasionally they do lose a job, but within a year they usually get a comparable one. The rest of us usually have to think of alternatives to life in large organizations. Being an entrepreneur is one option, but it isn't for everyone.

WHAT IS AN ENTREPRENEUR?

When I was young and growing up in Ohio, my friends and I wondered how Mr. Kokoski, who owned the carpet store, got to own a carpet store. Why didn't he just have a job like our dads? Entrepreneurs were odd ducks back then.

Being an entrepreneur is no longer unique or a mystery. There has been plenty written about all the phases of starting, funding, and growing a business. Major business schools offer courses in becoming an entrepreneur. There is also a growing number of resources on-line. If you key in *entrepreneur* in a search engine like Infoseek, there will be hundreds of thousands of entries. For example, you can get online and find out if you have the right stuff to be an entrepreneur. For a free, interactive entrepreneur profile, key in http://www.electsuccess.com.

If you key in http://www.avce.com, you can list a summary of your business plan for possible investors to review.

HARD TO PREDICT SUCCESS

Whether or not we should become entrepreneurs and whether we will be successful in our venture are hard to predict. Tom Kulzer, editor of the *Eclectro-MLM Digest*, suggests that there are five major characteristics of entrepreneurs:

- Being a problem solver. Entrepreneurs usually have the ability to find solutions for hard problems.
- Being a calculated risk taker. Entrepreneurs can assess risk accurately and recognize the importance of researching a subject.
- Being an innovator. Entrepreneurs are brimming with ideas and like to start companies to carry them out. Then they may sell the company once the idea is implemented.
- Being able to delegate. Entrepreneurs know how to hand over responsibility for work.
- Being able to process rejection and believe in themselves. Entrepreneurs usually think out of the box, and their line of thought will be unfamiliar to many people, ranging from family members to creditors. The puzzled looks, however, don't bother them.[4]

I know entrepreneurs who don't fit Kulzer's profile, however, and they're very successful. To illustrate, a buttoned-down man my age bought a printing franchise. He was never creative. He doesn't put in killer hours. He's also full of self-doubt. Nevertheless, he has a very successful business. His shop frequently wins first place in sales for the region. He'll probably open other branches of his shop in a number of locations throughout the state.

Then there was a communications professional at IBM. He was imaginative and shrewd. From his house of worship he had a lot of connections in business. He understood the graphics business and formed a partnership with an expert in graphics. But the business folded. Those who watched this disaster observed that this man, who was from a large organization, didn't know how to sell to smaller organizations. He gave the kind of pitch to a mom-and-pop deli that he would have given to General Motors.

From my experience, I am convinced that there are any number of personality types who become successful entrepreneurs. Entrepreneurs come in many different packages.

FAILURE AS PART OF SUCCESS

Many entrepreneurs fail on their way to success. Each year, according to *Inc.* magazine, about seventy thousand businesses fail.[5] A lot of these are first, second, and third tries by entrepreneurs. Mark Moore lost three businesses: two automobile repair shops and one software development venture. Then he founded TIS, a niche service that provides information to landlords about potential renters. TIS now grosses $1 million annually.

JUST ASK

There are ways to increase the odds that we will succeed. At *Inc.* magazine there's a saying: "Just ask." Entrepreneurs and potential entrepreneurs learn very quickly that their best source of information is other entrepreneurs, both those who succeeded and those who failed. In my experience, I've found entrepreneurs to be very generous with their time.

Before I started my public relations firm, I went right to the horse's mouth—other public relations agencies. The owners of these agencies would eventually be my competition, yet they were straight with me, and helpful. They answered every one of my questions ranging from the importance of the location of the office to what kind of salaries to pay. They also told me that having a business would be hard on my family, since I would be preoccupied. They explained that it's imperative to select your clients—those who give you the most trouble will probably only contribute 20 percent of your revenues.

Other entrepreneurs will also share their mistakes with you. One, who was still blushing, confessed that she used to charge too little. She found that such a mistake is irreversible. She could never get her clients to pay her the market value, so she had to dump those clients.

Another common mistake she made was assuming that she needed a partner. In her case, a partner was more trouble than a help. In a partnership, it's common for each partner to assume that she's doing the most work.

All this candid information from public relations experts scared the life out of me. But I wanted to try it—I wanted to have my own public relations agency—and my family was supportive of my dream. Also, people with whom I had worked previously in a large organization were willing to join my new business.

In return for their generosity I frequently refer appropriate business to the public relations agencies that gave me advice. Although we're competition, we root for each other.

It also pays to go to the horse's mouth when buying a franchise. A franchise is a structured business, like McDonald's or Weight Watchers. The price of entry varies between a low cost of $10,000 and $1 million, and owners of the franchise regularly have to give a percentage of the profits back to the parent company. How strict the rules governing the operation of the franchise are varies with the franchise.

About forty thousand franchises are started each year, and 40 percent are started by outplaced executives.[7] You can do research on franchises and come across, for example, the negative article about the Subway food franchises that appeared several years ago in the *Wall Street Journal*, but the best information comes from those who already have a franchise.

A friend of mine was thinking of buying a frozen yogurt franchise. The owner of one such franchise told him that the product was good but his location was bad. Eventually he moved the business and did well. My friend immediately "got it" that location was important.

From owners of franchises we can also find out how short a leash the company keeps on its franchises, if they sponsor too many in one geographical location, and what employee turnover in the business is like.

OTHER RESOURCES

There is now an almost infinite number of resources available to those who think they might want to become entrepreneurs. Which of these prove most helpful depends on how we learn. Some people learn best experientially, while others learn better from books. Here are some of the resources we can look into:

EXPERIENCE

There is that old saying: Learn on the company. People who have worked all their careers in corporate public relations might find it useful to work a few years for a public relations agency before starting one of their own. They'll see firsthand how to get new clients, what happens when a client departs, the plight of having too much work, and the stress of purchasing decisions such as buying new office equipment.

You can also get solid experience as a volunteer. A woman in her forties wanted to become a clinical social worker with a private practice. Before she went to school for two years for a master's degree in social work, she volunteered on a suicide hot line, where she found out that she didn't like to deal with people in crisis. She looked into other types of self-employment and bought a candy franchise.

THE FEDS

The Small Business Administration (SBA) can be a gold mine. In the *SBA Hotline Answer Book*, Gustav Berle points out that the SBA hot line (800-827-5722) gets about 250,000 calls a year. This is a very good place for an entrepreneur to start hunting around for information.[8] It's also good for questions about funding and how to grow a business that is flat.

There's an SBA in Washington, D.C., but there are also ninety SBA filing offices around the country. The SBA hot line will give you the number of the field office nearest you, or you can check the government pages of your telephone directory.

A group which works closely with the SBA is the Service Corps of Retired Executives (SCORE). SCORE, with 380 chapters in the U.S. and territories, consists of high-powered executives who give their advice free of charge. They're retired, but still want a hand in the business world. The Small Business Investment Corporation (SBIC) makes funds available and also provides management expertise.

In addition to the SBA, there are myriad other resources available from the government. These can be especially useful for those considering an import-export business. Check the book *Free Help From Uncle Sam to Start Your Own Business (or Expand the One You Have).*⁹

The government is also available on-line. Contact the U.S. Business Advisor at http://www.business.gov.

SCHOOL

In almost every college-level educational institution, from Harvard Business School to Norwalk Community College, there are classes, seminars, and one-day crash courses on starting and managing your own business. If you are used to learning in a school environment, this may be the place for you.

The pitfall here is the level of sophistication of the institution. Maybe you have been investigating starting a travel agency for over ten years. You already know everything from tax deductions to how many Americans travel to Italy in the winter. In many of the classes offered on entrepreneurship, you would be bored. Contact the instructor ahead of time to find out what will be covered and what level of knowledge is assumed.

There are those among us who will want the whole enchilada: an academic degree in entrepreneurship. Think twice. The research doesn't show that those with degrees in starting and managing their own businesses are more successful than those who learn by doing. If you want to find out about running a greeting card store, get a job at the local Hallmark. You probably don't need a master's degree.

BOOKS

There are plenty of books on entrepreneurship in general, and special businesses such as pet sitting. Most of those are well researched. A friend of mine who loves animals ordered a few books on pet sitting from Amazon.com and found them very helpful. One even advised her what to charge. Since she was between jobs she decided to try it. She found out that it was an awful lot of work for $12 a visit. The books didn't depict this enterprise as so labor intensive.

Reading about a business is light years away from actually running one. Also, by the time a business is examined in books, demand for its product or service might have peaked. Entrepreneurs have to be alert to emerging trends before there's a saturation of the market.

MAGAZINES

About two decades ago, *Inc.*, the magazine for small business, was alone in that category. Today there are tons of magazines for entrepreneurs, both in print and on-line. How useful they are depends on what we want from them. Some are essentially motivational, while others give in-depth information on subjects ranging from getting funding to getting out of a franchise agreement. One advantage magazines have over books is their timeliness.

THE CORE COMPETENCE

In a small business, entrepreneurs have to have a very clear idea what they're doing. We have to ask ourselves, "What business are we in?" How we answer the question will depend on our strengths, skills, and resources—that is, our core competence. McDonald's sells fast food, but its core competence is providing customers with predictability, convenience, and value. Planet Hollywood sells food, but its core competence used to be providing customers with the experience of dining with celebrities. Not too many celebrities have shown up recently, however, and Planet Hollywood's stock is way down. The core competence of my insurance agent is to sell peace of mind; the policy is only the vehicle through which that peace comes. In my line of work, my core competence is providing information in the form the client wants it. Placing stories in the *New York Times* or holding a special event in the heart of Chicago are only tools that I use.

We each have to decide what it is we really do. If that's not clear to us, it won't be clear to clients and customers. Our core competence is the "guts" of our business.

PACKAGING

Just as important as the substance, or guts, of our business is its image. If we create and reinforce the right image for our business, we're half of the way to success. If Kellogg hadn't created the right image for its cereals, it would never have become a global brand name. Would Coca-Cola have become Coca-Cola without some very adept image making?

For those new at image making, it's useful to model the image of the business on the image of another business that is doing well. Analyze how that company communicates a certain image. For example, what does Disney say and do to get the message across that its product is happiness? What is the company doing that might hurt that image? What could be done to improve it?

We can learn a great deal about image by going to the business section of the bookstore and finding books and chapters of books on brand names. Key in *brand name* on an Internet search engine and you'll come up with some interesting stuff. It's also helpful to walk through the aisles of stores and analyze what a brand name says about the product.

RESEARCHING THE MARKET

There are books, reference libraries, courses, and advice from the SBA to help you research your market. You can also read up·on how to conduct focus groups and find out what consumers think about your idea. If you're going for funding, you'll probably have to write a formal business plan.

If this work is too much for you, you can hire consultants who will do some or all of it. There are people who are great at researching an idea but can't write up the material. They'll call up a communications temporary employment agency to contract a writer. Some people don't know how to position their material so that it will attract investors. They can contract an investor relations specialist to put together the data in such a way that Wall Street will bite.

However, research isn't just something to get done and over with. It's during this process that you find out if your concept is viable. One corporate refugee did a business plan based on selling public relations services on a sliding scale to nonprofit organizations. She also ran focus groups about how nonprofits would perceive her services and found out that nonprofits would devalue her service because it was discount priced. She dropped the idea.

JUMPING IN

One of my vendors sat for years at her desk at a major corporation thinking about how nice it would be to be a freelance writer. She calculated how much she would save on clothes and nylons by working from home. She knew she could get freelance clients by answering some of the many part-time help wanted ads under "Writer" and "Public Relations" in the *New York Times*, and she spoke to several of her colleagues about helping her out with the writing during peak times.

Then this woman was downsized. She went into shock. No one is really prepared to lose a job, no matter how much fantasizing they've done about "freedom." She went on a few full-time job interviews to see if she could stand life in one more corporation but couldn't find a fit. So she jumped in and freelanced, but only $3,000 in work came in during the first six months. What she saved on attire went into keeping the heat at seventy degrees all day. (It never occurred to her that she would have to keep the heat up all day long now that she was home.) The gigs in the *New York Times* didn't pay squat. When the work did come in, it came in unevenly. It was feast or famine. When it was a feast, she would be busy briefing someone else to help her with the assignments. So self-employment wasn't utopia. She did stick with it, but she advises acquaintances to think long and hard before opening a business.

Even those who are well prepared experience shock and disorientation when launching a business. In *Out on Your Own: From Corporate to Self-Employment*, Robert Bly and Gary Blake point out how hard the adjustment is. One of the big down factors is isolation. Yes, we may be our own boss, but we no longer have a roomful of colleagues to talk with. Some entrepreneurs find it useful to rent offices in buildings where there are a lot of people to socialize with. The other difficult feeling is the haunting sense that we don't have a "real" job.[10] It takes years to realize that being self-employed is okay.

The trick is to hang in there long enough to become comfortable with what you're doing. I know of colleagues who have tried self-employment for a few months, but the isolation and lack of business got to them and they ran back to corporate jobs.

Incidentally, frequently when the failed entrepreneur returns to the corporate fold, the reception is chilly. A recent article in *Inc.* explains that those who try the corporate route again are sometimes treated like untouchables. They tend not to get good jobs because the savvy in the corporate world know that once they get their confidence back and bills paid, they'll probably quit and try another entrepreneurial venture.[11]

One scared entrepreneur who's making excellent money began her venture with the idea that she would give it two years. She viewed it as an experiment and handled her mistakes as learning experiences.

Within eighteen months of start-up the business took off. Was she tempted to run back to the corporate world? You bet. But she made that two-year commitment.

MEASURING SUCCESS

New entrepreneurs must continually measure how they're doing. The problem is that since they're new at this, they might not know what the numbers mean. Here it's imperative to network with other entrepreneurs in your field. Revenues of $90,000 for the first year may seem great to a freelance human resources consultant, but by networking, she might find out that she could be making $250,000. Her problem is that she's not charging enough. Again, by networking, she can find out average rates.

The meaning of measurements probably will change over time. Economic conditions, more experience—they all influence how we'll do.

BAILING OUT

With a troubled business, one of the hardest decisions to make is whether to hang in there. When I was working on my book, *The Critical Fourteen Years of Your Professional Life*, I asked George Gendron, editor in chief of *Inc.*, about this. He sees two reasons for bailing out. One is that you've lost faith in the enterprise. Here it doesn't matter what your investors or customers think; it's what *you* think. If you don't believe in the concept anymore, then maybe it's time to close shop. The other reason for walking away is if the problems of the business are destructive to your personal life.[12] I think what Gendron is really saying is that we are the only ones who can decide to pull the plug.

STARTING OVER

Following a failure, most entrepreneurs will try again—and again. On the other hand, there are those who have been seduced by the hype of entrepreneurship. When they fail, they will give up. It's this second group who has the hardest time recovering from a setback. They're the ones in the company cafeteria who tell you about their failed business—whether you're interested or not. It seems that the only way for them to lift this cloud is for them to have a significant success at their jobs. The lesson here is clear: If you're only dabbling in entrepreneurship, do it part time and without giving up your day job. A full-time failure can be very hard on the soul.

JACK O'DWYER

Jack O'Dwyer has been a global brand name in public relations for years. His mission has been to keep public relations professionals, their organizations, and the media up-to-date on what's happening in communications. In 1968, O'Dwyer started writing a weekly newsletter about public relations. That was the beginning of J. R. O'Dwyer Company, Inc. Since then, O'Dwyer has added three directories, which have become the bibles of public relations. One gives information about corporate public relations departments; another about public relations agencies; and a third about who's who in the field. In addition, O'Dwyer publishes job listings and a magazine called *O'Dwyer's PR Services Report*, which has the largest circulation of any magazine covering public relations. Besides his publications, O'Dwyer informally serves the public relations community by functioning as a key source of fast, reliable, authoritative information about the profession.

Thirty years ago, O'Dwyer was ahead of his time by recognizing how valuable up-to-date information could be. Since then, he's made millions from that idea.

* * *

INTERVIEW WITH JACK O'DWYER

RD: Jack, part of your genius was seeing that there was a need for your kind of information services. That's what entrepreneurship is all about.

JO: Genius? I don't know. People urged me to cover public relations because there was void there. What I did right was listen to them.

RD: Why did you become an entrepreneur?

JO: I had been a daily newspaper reporter for fourteen years and a business reporter for ten. My specialty was public relations and advertising. When people called to my attention that there was a need for comprehensive, accurate coverage of public relations, I saw that I could fill it by starting my own business.

RD: What were the challenges?

JO: Well, to find people who would subscribe to my newsletter. You might say I had been preparing for that all my career by getting to know a lot of people and doing favors for them. When I set myself up in business, many of them bought a subscription.

RD: What are the challenges of running a successful business?

JO: Actually, there haven't been any major challenges. I have plenty of friends in the field, and they help me gather information. For backup, I hired a certified public accountant.

RD: What advice do you have for people thinking about becoming entrepreneurs?

JO: Do a lot of favors for people and they, in turn, will help you. As for capital, you need about six months' pay in your pocket before you start out.

RD: What advice would you give to discouraged entrepreneurs?

JO: Get to know more potential customers and find out their needs.

RD: What are the important tools in your work today?

JO: Technology is now key. Computers, cell phones, call forwarding, paging, Web sites—they all help get new business, and all this technology can be used to promote, promote, and promote at a low cost. You get high visibility in an affordable way, no matter what business you're in.

* * *

Now You Know...

- If you're finding it hard getting a conventional job, starting your own business is an option.
- Starting a business isn't for everyone.

- The best preparation for starting a business is to ask other entrepreneurs about their businesses.
- Learn the basics about an industry by working for others.
- Model the structure of your business on other successful businesses.
- Develop an image or brand-name for the business and keep reinforcing it.
- Losing a business is traumatic. Be sure entrepreneurship is what you want.

10

THE PAST *DOES* MATTER—IF WE KNOW HOW TO HANDLE IT

If past history was all there was to the game, the richest people would be the librarians.

—Warren Buffett

What Do I Do?

- The job I had with a big-name manufacturer in the 1970s was very formative in my development as a marketer, but I'm afraid to mention that experience because people might think that I'm stuck in time.
- I have three homes, and years ago my parents only had one—a trailer—but when I talk about how it used to be, people get those glazed-over looks.
- At meetings I want to bring up my experience working for Lee Iacocca, but I feel like then I date myself.
- Management consultant Peter Drucker alludes to the past and he gets quoted. If I do that, I get told to move on.

THE PAST IS REAL

After a downsizing at an aerospace company, someone from an outplacement firm got up on the stage and told those booted out to move on with their lives. It was as if those twenty or thirty years spent with the company hadn't existed, as if the employees' personal and professional past hadn't included this particular company.

So much in contemporary life gives us messages to suppress our sense of history. A new regime comes to Company X and we "get it" that we're not supposed to ever allude to the former regime. To survive, we pretend to live in the here and now.

However, the past *was* real. It contains information which can help us in the present and the future. It's part of our identity, both professional and personal. But our past can become a liability if we don't handle it right. We all know those in our profession who constantly talk about "how it used to be." After a while, everyone ignores them.

THE PAST AS AN ASSET

A Kennedy such as Joe or John gets up on the podium and invokes the legacy of John and Bobby Kennedy, and many of us get chills down our spine. For the Kennedys, much of the past has been an asset, and they use it well.

In the bestselling *The Discipline of Market Leaders*, Michael Treacy and Fred Wiersema discuss the history of AT&T's Universal Card, Intel, and Airborne Express to make points about marketing principles.[1] They show that there's an immediate tie between the history they're discussing and how to become more successful. The authors are using the past as a tool.

In *Managing for the Future*, management consultant Peter Drucker analyzes the corporate culture in terms of examples from the past, such as what Konrad Adenauer did in Germany in the 1920s.[2] Part of Drucker's reputation comes from his ability to dig back into the past and make it useful for looking at the present and future.

Cable television is making a fortune showing old sitcoms and old movies. In an age of uncertainty, people like the reassurance that the past offers. On *I Love Lucy*, Lucy will always be a flake, determined to break into show business. In *The Wizard of Oz*, Dorothy will always get back home. That certainty contrasts with our reality. We never know what China will do next. Will the Fed raise or lower interest rates? Will a cure for prostate cancer be discovered in our lifetime?

THE PAST AS A LIABILITY

For every Drucker who brilliantly uses the past as a multidimensional tool, there are millions of professionals who shoot themselves in the foot every time they step out of the present. There are employees working at IBM who still talk about how it used to be at the old IBM. They'll never get anywhere in the new IBM.

There was one human disaster I'll call Bob. Bob was fortunate enough to get an excellent education at Harvard University—and he went on scholarship. He was also lucky enough to work for great companies when they were really making tracks in the sand. Bob will eagerly share with you the philosophy of education at Harvard. He can also tell you all about how it was being part of the team at Company X or Y, which were constantly covered in the business media. When Bob lost his last job he got interviews, his résumé was strong—but he didn't get a comparable job. All his anecdotes about the past hung him.

A man in the legal department of a major corporation had a serious accident years ago. He dates time from that accident. Everyone around him senses something is "wrong." The man is obviously stuck in time.

HANDLE WITH CARE

The past can date us and lead people to have reservations about us. The other day a freelance writer came in to see me about getting possible assignments. He mentioned a few companies he had done work for during the 1980s. I wondered why he was talking about the past and not primarily focusing on the present. That showed poor presentation skills on his part. I concluded that he couldn't write presentations for his clients.

Résumés come across my desk every day, and it baffles me that professionals in their forties go into detail about what extracurricular activities they participated in at college. To me that's a red flag that the present didn't turn out as well as they had expected.

HOW HE SEES THE PAST—RICHARD BROCKMAN, M.D.

Richard Brockman is a man of medicine, but also a man of the world. A psychiatrist, Dr. Brockman approaches his profession as a Renaissance man. He has published articles in the *International Journal of*

Psychoanalysis, General Hospital Psychiatry, The Atlantic Monthly, and the *Los Angeles Times Magazine.* He's as interested in psychotropic medication as he is in some of the spiritually-based healing approaches practiced in central India.

Dr. Brockman is currently on the staff of Columbia-Presbyterian Medical Center in New York. He had previously worked at Mount Sinai Medical Center in New York; Kino Community Hospital in Tucson, Arizona; the Alfred Adler Mental Hygiene Clinic in New York; and the Phoenix House Drug Rehabilitation Center, also in New York. He has lectured widely on subjects, ranging from reality and certainty to trauma and the homeless.

* * *

INTERVIEW WITH DR. RICHARD BROCKMAN

RD: In *A Christmas Carol,* Scrooge gets lucky: He's able to experience the past, present, and future, and that experience changes him. Not many of us are that fortunate. We have the past and the present, but we don't know how to use them as tools, and because of that we rarely have a good handle on what might happen in the future. Why aren't we able to use time better to make us more successful professionally and have a fuller personal life?

RB: Our culture doesn't have an appropriate reverence for the value of time, which, alas, is a finite gift for all of us. At this stage in capitalism's development, many of us are preoccupied with money, and the need to get it, which keeps us rooted in the present. At the top of our conscious mind is a passion for how to get money today. Often we "keep score" on our lives by measuring how well we have done in our financial affairs. You might say that a "bad year" might be one in which we didn't make all the money we wished to make.

RD: Are there factors besides capitalism that keep us rooted in the present?

RB: Yes, another key factor is the pace of our lives. Everything is moving so quickly that we feel we have to rush just to keep up with the present. I think that this pace frightened many people and they are seeking a sense of comfort by staying within themselves. We're seeing more and more people focused on themselves and their little islands of concern rather than on larger issues.

RD: I know what you're saying. For many of us, it has become hard just to get through the day—on time. So, how can we break away from "present-ness" and self-preoccupation and use the past better?

RB: The answer is balance. It's an old answer, but it applies in spades today. There *are* other things in life besides making a living. There are ways to slow down our reality and still survive in the digital age. There are entities outside ourselves that can engross us. Maybe we can become interested in world peace or improving the schools in our communities.

    We all have to work hard at getting and maintaining balance. The first step is to become self-aware—aware of ourselves and what kind of life we are living.

RD: How do we become self-aware?

RB: There are a number of ways. One is psychotherapy. Therapy can help us become sensitive to the kind of life we're living. Another way is to become aware of history. Where do certain ideas come from? When did we first think of medicine as a science? If we look at life through the perspective of history, we'll see ourselves and our immediate world more clearly. Knowing the history of medicine helps me be a better practitioner today.

RD: But whenever we look into the past, isn't there always the danger of regret? Doesn't someone who has regrets turn other people off? I don't want to interview someone for a job in our firm who says, "I regret not going into agency work earlier."

RB: Regret can be a useful tool. Being aware of what we didn't like in the past can help us understand what we want right now. It can also help us shape the choices we make today. In society, there are times and places to talk about our regrets and there are times to stay strictly in the present. Regret can become problematic if it gets out of balance. For instance, excessive regret can lead to depression, and guilt.

    What each of us has to learn is how to use our personal past and the history of the world creatively. For example, as we change our interpretation of the past might change. It's fun to look at those changes, and examining the past is a way of getting out of ourselves in the present. Creative use of the past can not only improve our performance as professionals, it can help us become better human beings.

* * *

CREATIVE USE OF THE PAST

Dr. Brockman advocates creative use of the past—our own past and history in a larger sense. He's not alone. Many educational institutions offer courses in how to retrieve and make sense of one's past. More and more families are writing and publishing their histories. That kind of exercise helps us understand how we came to be who we are and what possibilities are out there for us now and in the future. A friend of mine is considering buying a fast food franchise. He's studying the history of McDonald's to determine where the pitfalls might be.

As for history in general, we're becoming more sensitive to the fact that the past can help guide our decisions in the present and for the future. The most recent example of that has been the stock market. In the third quarter of 1998, the stock market went through convulsions. The panic wasn't more widespread because many of us reached back in time to the crash of 1987. Every money show on cable alluded to that history. It was made clear that the market recovered in about fifteen months.

In 1985, if IBM had explored what happens to leading companies that become complacent, the company might not have gone through such tough times in the early 1990s, when its stock plunged from about 172 to the 40s.

OUR PERSONAL PAST—PUTTING TOGETHER
NEW IDENTITIES

Reaching back into our own past can help us change in ways that will let us be more successful and happier today. To make a comeback, actor John Travolta needed a different identity than the one he had when he had made *Saturday Night Fever*.

In *New Passages*, Gail Sheehy observes, "A single fixed identity is a liability today."[3] The Barbara Walters of twenty years ago is not the Barbara Walters of today.

On the other hand, the actress Jane Fonda changed too much as she moved toward sixty years of age. She gave up the actress side of herself when she married media tycoon Ted Turner. There are rumors that she's now unhappy with that identity. Fonda has an excellent track record for changing her identity when she needs to. You can bet money that she will come through this passage well.

Former child star Patty Duke has been able to put together a comeback in the entertainment world because she keeps changing her identity. She currently plays older roles with grace and passion. Incidentally, Duke wrote a book about her past called *A Brilliant Madness*. It was well received, and obviously helped her deal with her regrets and aging.[4] The book was also a public service. She was able to use her own life history and struggle with a bipolar condition to educate readers about treatments for bipolar disease. This is the kind of outward look Brockman recommends.

OUR PERSONAL PAST—BECOMING A DIGGER

A colleague in his fifties came to me and wondered who he had been in the early 1960s when he was eighteen and applying to colleges. Why hadn't he applied to the top tier of colleges such as Harvard, Yale, or Amherst? Why hadn't he even *tried* to get in? Instead, he had gone to a small college in western Pennsylvania. I told him that he would have to dig to find out.

This man, whom I'll call Bart, phoned his roommate from his freshman year in college and asked him what kind of person he had been then. He also called some acquaintances from high school, and an aunt. With them, he explored the question: Who was I at eighteen?

What Bart discovered was that at eighteen he was quaking in his boots, afraid of the world, afraid of competition, afraid of being challenged. That information has helped him take better advantage of the time he has now. Now Bart takes more risks, which makes him more visible at work. He vows he'll never underachieve again.

We can change who we are if we recognize how we were shaped in the past. Jack Johnson, an accountant, knows that the person he is now isn't a valuable commodity in the work place. He's too rigid. It would help him to look into his past to see how he has previously handled change. If he studies that he'll become more aware of what he could be doing to accommodate change in the workplace today.

Most of us don't need to invest a lot of money in tracing our roots. A few phone calls should start the ball rolling. Recently, a client, a CEO of a consumer-products company, wondered why he couldn't enjoy all that he had achieved. He called a few aunts, a few cousins, people from the old neighborhood who were still living. He was able to piece together that while he was growing up, his family and neighbors had a dark view of life. They were very fearful that they were going to lose the little that they had, so they tended not to enjoy their success. After this digging, this executive gave himself permission to relax and like his life.

You might travel to find insight about your past. One vendor I use decided to return to the place where she grew up. Over the years, she had received criticism about being "too direct." As she went to stores in her old town and ate in restaurants, she realized that the culture of the town was pretty blunt. There was little grace attached to social interaction. Be seeing how being "too direct" sounded, she was able to polish her social skills.

It can also be useful to investigate what was going on in the larger world during important periods of our lives. This puts our personal history into a larger context. A colleague used to regret wasting so much time in graduate school. When she researched that time frame she found out that the best and brightest didn't go directly to work from college during that era; they went to graduate school. Her choice to go on to graduate school was an appropriate choice at the time, and now she no longer complains about it.

To move forward, you might have to go back.

THAT STUFF CALLED THE HISTORY OF THE WORLD

On a professional level, understanding the past can also be an asset, but we have to present this information in a way that doesn't label us as stuck in the past. In his talk to the troops, an executive at a consumer-products company explained why too much innovation in food products never worked. He gave examples such as soft cookies. He analyzed how conservative people are about what goes into their mouths, and then moved from the past to the present. He didn't dwell on interesting aspects of history; he used just enough history to make his point.

I was at a meeting with executives from an energy company who wanted to increase sales of petroleum. Someone brought up the promotions used at gas stations in the 1970s. She made her point briefly, citing statistics about how promotions increased sales. Her stock in the company went up.

Of course, there are those who make a terrible impression when the allude to the past. They talk about the past for its own sake and not as a tool to illuminate the present. Since this data doesn't add to anyone's information bank, these chroniclers are usually perceived as out of touch. They're frequently negative. They assert how good the past was and how bad the present is. They portray the history of the company as a series of screwups. They remind employees about the early mistakes an executive made.

If we are fascinated with the past, let's call that a hobby and keep its pleasures to ourselves.

A CHECKLIST FOR REACHING BACK INTO THE PAST

The past, whether it's our own or the history of the world, can be tricky business. It has to be handled with skill. Here is a checklist to keep in mind before you start talking about the past.

THE AUDIENCE

Is this audience interested in data from the past or will you be seen as having a lack of focus?

Two associates and I went to an investment bank looking for new business. The group who received us was in their late twenties. It was clear that they didn't want to hear about the history of my work; they just wanted to be informed about recent results.

TIME CONSTRAINT

If clients want a speech turned out in a day, they probably aren't emotionally geared to hear about how Peggy Noonan wrote speeches for former president Ronald Reagan. Clients will feel more comfortable about the project getting done on deadline if we stay in the present.

LESS IS MORE

Because we are so used to the "sound bite" information of television, we get easily restless if too much data is being thrown at us.

Before we cite a personal anecdote from the past or an anecdote about the history of the coal industry, we should boil it down to the essential parts. If I want to tell you about how it was growing up in Ohio in the 1950s, I can probably skip all the details about what happened to my fourth grade teacher, Mrs. Sklar.

There are courses available that help us frame our stories so that people enjoy them. In Dale Carnegie seminars, we can be trained to deliver our stories within three minutes.

NO EXPECTATIONS

Not all parts of the past play equally well. There is no guarantee that an anecdote or fact that engages us will capture the attention of others. So we can protect ourselves by presenting our stories in a low-key fashion, without obvious expectations.

There was an executive from an aerospace firm who delivered a speech about mission. With great solemnity, he talked about how medieval towns viewed the construction of a cathedral. No one in the audience reacted. That particular analogy meant nothing to them. This executive should have tried this anecdote on a group of people before the speech.

HISTORY IS A STRETCH

In our culture, most of us seek immediate accessibility, not historical precedents. We want to find out about remedies for headaches by walking the aisles of the pharmacy. Most of us don't want to look up how headaches were cured in ancient Greece. If we recognize that in our culture, reaching back into the past is a stretch, we'll be selective about what information from the past we share.

Now You Know...

- The past can be a powerful tool or a liability; it depends on how you handle it.
- Digging into your personal past can help you change and become happier and more successful.
- History has many lessons for the professional world.
- In using the past, less is often more.

11

BEYOND WORK

For many people, work is a central driving force....But it's the outside interests, even passions, that help lend balance and spice to their lives.

—Robert McAllister, "Labors of Love"

What Do I Do?

- I tried to network, but I had nothing to talk about except my work.
- I went to a job interview. They asked me about my hobbies. I had nothing to say.
- Work doesn't have the pull on me that it once did.
- I'm happier working with my model trains than I am going to my job.

GETTING BALANCE AGAIN

Remember back in high school, how *they* told us about balance? *They* told us that if we didn't hit the books all the time, but also played in the band and worked on the school newspaper, we would become well-rounded? Being well-rounded, *they* explained, would make it easier for us to get into a good college and then be hired by a top corporation. I believed them and threw myself into extracurricular activities. I was Mr. School Spirit.

What *they* were trying to get us to understand was the importance of being involved and having social skills. Soon enough we saw that for ourselves. In college, "teacher's pet" wasn't necessarily the brightest student in class. The pet was the student who knew how to engage the professor's attention. Later, on the job, the person who got promoted wasn't the hardest worker; it was the person who could talk easily about anything with anyone. That same person usually had a lot of interests, ranging from sports to the theater to a collection of 1950s Cadillacs. He, or she, never let work trump everything else. For instance, no matter how busy he was closing the books at the end of the month, he was never abrupt with you or made you feel like a pest.

EMOTIONAL INTELLIGENCE

Around 1995, Daniel Goleman provided research to support the old notion that it's our broad involvement in this thing called "life" and our social skills that get us ahead, not what's in our head. In *Emotional Intelligence*, he explained clearly why sometimes the B students get to be vice presidents of DuPont instead of the A students.[1]

One way we develop emotional intelligence is through common interests. In my office, many of us watch football on Monday night. When we come into work the next day, we talk about it, and that's how we win friends and influence people. Bonds form. People get to know what we're all about. Those who don't get involved in any of our conversations have less impact on the company and in our lives. We don't bond with them. They rarely get ahead. They're too busy working.

WORK AS NUMBER ONE

Somewhere along the way, many of us forgot the lessons of high school. We made work number one in our lives. Maybe some boss praised us for working so hard. Maybe we just felt more comfortable hiding in work rather than having a life. So we worked through lunch instead of inviting folks to dinner to bond and get the gossip. We stopped going skiing. We no longer read for pleasure. Even our families gradually took second place to work.

Inevitably, we watched the less gifted but well-rounded workers get the promotions, open their businesses, and buy million-dollar houses. Maybe in some distant galaxies nerds get ahead, but not in the circles I travel. In those circles, you better have something other than work to talk about at dinner parties and on the company jet with the senior vice president. Successful people always know that it's inappropriate to talk about work all the time.

YOUNG AND BORING VERSUS OLDER AND BORING

Young, so-called cubicle rats are usually left alone to do their work. They get a lot done and don't bother anyone. But an older cubicle rat is an embarrassment: Aging rats make the department seem older than it is. They have nothing to talk about except work. They're self-righteous because they put in fourteen-hour days. And the boss usually keeps them hidden from the brass and customers. Eventually, the rats get caught in some kind of corporate trap and are history.

At the former NYNEX, Doug Mello was interested in everyone and everything. He asked about good books to read, and he happily bragged about his wife, who was an attorney, and his son, who got into an Ivy League school. When Mello's division was dissolved, he went on to an even better job. At that job he spent more time talking in the hall with colleagues then he did hunched over his desk. His staff loved him.

At IBM, Bill Blankenship was a good corporate soldier by day and novelist by night. One of his books, *Brotherly Love*, was made into a movie. By all measures, Blankenship was one of the most content workers at IBM. Some speculate that his contentment with his job was the result of the creative release he had at night.

GET A HOBBY

Experts in employability are telling us to get outside interests if we want to become more marketable. If you're over forty, it's time to stop working so obsessively and develop some interests off the job that are not work-related and are simply pursued for pure pleasure, enjoyment, or intellectual growth. According to the trade magazine *Playthings*, the hobby industry is now posing stiff competition to video games, television, and video cassettes. For instance, model kits are now almost a $100 million business.[2] More and more people are "getting it" that work isn't enough for a life. There's even a proliferation of articles in the media, such as those in *Nation's Business*, on how to turn hobbies into businesses of second or third careers.[3]

Recently the *Wall Street Journal* carried an article about stockbroker Ted Lipinski, who blasts off in a rented fighter jet to get his mind completely off work.[4] More and more harried workers—be they executives or rank-and-file—are taking up extreme hobbies like jetting around or bungee jumping to get relief from the strain of work. On many jobs today there is reduced staff, which means that we have to function as leaders. We frequently learn a lot about leadership from our outside interests, be it being a parent or coach of Little League.

ADVICE FROM OUTPLACEMENT

In chapter 8, I interviewed career services guru Steve Harrison, president of Lee Hecht Harrison. He has been the point person for the firm's growth and global expansion. Harrison is convinced that older employees who don't develop interests other than work are putting themselves at a disadvantage in today's job market.

* * *

INTERVIEW WITH STEVE HARRISON, PART TWO

RD: Why are outside interests so important for older workers?

SH: When prospective employers find out that older workers have more going for them than just their focus on the job, they can see that these workers have kept engaged in life. In fact, I advise job candidates to volunteer that they are passionate about some interest, such as music, art, tennis or even fly-fishing. Why do successful people talk so much about their golf game? They know that it indicates that they have more in life than their jobs. At the same time, they are aware that business is often done on golf courses. When older workers don't have interests it's easy for employers to assume that they're tired.

RD: I guess what you're saying is that outside interests can neutralize the age factor.

SH: Yes. The burden is on us to refute an employer's idea that older workers don't have drive and energy.

RD: What kind of activities do you pursue?

SH: I was having fun fly-fishing long before Robert Redford's *A River Runs Through It*. I am a great believer in physical fitness. I set up a whole gym in our house and use it regularly. My family is relatively young, and I make sure that I'm very involved with them. I enjoy playing tennis and distance running.

RD: How does having outside interests affect your attitude?

SH: Attitude is a wholistic thing. If you are balanced about the work part of your life, you're going to have perspective on finding and keeping a job. For example, you will see that in many fields there is a shortage of skilled workers. Employers need you. They also need to hold on to you. This perspective helps you deal from a position of strength. Perspective also helps prevent depression. There's really nothing to get depressed about. You have to have the attitude that you need a job and will therefore find one.

In the new marketplace, employers want you to be able to make a contribution from day one. They want to see that you have confidence, that you know your worth. When you have interests other than work, you usually present yourself in a more confident manner.

RD: How else do outside interests help us?

SH: They give us an entree to networking. Golf, volunteer work, participating in marathons, collecting electric guitars—they all give us a chance to meet other people, and we have something in common with those people. I can't emphasize enough how important networking is to getting and holding jobs. Networking is also key in getting the inside information about starting a business.

RD: Does sharing an interest with the powers that be give you an advantage in the job market?

SH: It may. When you share an interest with someone you have a clearer idea about what makes him or her tick, and then it's easier to have empathy with that person. Connecting is primarily about empathy.

* * *

EXECUTIVES VERSUS NONACHIEVERS

When I started out in the work world in the 1960s, it was obvious even back then that the well-rounded get ahead. There was an obvious difference between the CEOs and the nonachievers. When you entered the offices of the CEOs, there was evidence of their hobbies on display. For some, it was a photo of a big fish or a photo of their family and friends in their boat. For others, it was a trophy from some type of athletic contest, or some collected model trains. There were also plaques from organizations such as the United Way expressing appreciation for volunteer activities. There was a collection of family pictures—right down to the grandchildren. The message was clear that these people did more than work. They knew how to enjoy the good life. We used to say that those leaders knew how to work hard and play hard.

For nonachievers, the ambience was very different. You'd be lucky to see a picture of the family. There was no indication that they had outside interests. They seemed so hurried that I doubted that they had any time to give to volunteer activities. Nonachievers usually remained stuck, and one day they woke up at fifty and realized that all that work had gotten them nowhere in the organization. Being a nonachiever is a sure strategy for ultimate failure.

A few of them did eventually wise up and stopped being little work robots. They used breaks and lunch to network. They developed interests and mentored younger people, and that gave them a built-in support group. They found causes for volunteer work—and then they started to climb the ladder. You, too, can start to become your own person and let the organization know that you have a life. Odds are that you will get more respect.

FAMILY AS GOLD MINE

With all the generations in a family, this group of people can be a gold mine in terms of our interests, getting us quickly up to speed on everything from the latest advances in bypass surgery to Girl Scout cookies. Families push us out of our usual comfort zone, and instead of CNN, we might watch *Melrose Place*. We stop talking about the Beatles and check out some newer groups.

Because family life can be so stimulating and rewarding, both men and women are arranging their work schedules to enable them to spend more time with family members, all three or four generations of them.

It's interesting to note that in Tom Wolfe's new novel *A Man in Full*, the sixty-year-old antihero Charlie Croker is losing hold of his financial empire, but he doesn't get support and nurturance from his family because it has never been important to him. Having no interest in family is one sign of Croker's spiritual decay.[5]

Millions of professionals have neglected their families, and then "saw the light" and were able to start rebuilding their relationships. There is no age discrimination when it comes to getting back into the family.

NOT ALL INTERESTS ARE CREATED EQUAL

A West Coast executive took a job in the Midwest. He certainly had a number of consuming interests. One of them was beekeeping. During lunch one day he took some of his colleagues to a dangerous part of town to get some equipment for his bees. Another of his interests was old trucks. He drove them to work. These interests went over like lead balloons. Because his interests were so off-beat in the Midwest, he couldn't connect. When his boss started a campaign to get rid of him, there was no chorus of support. Oddball, highly unconventional interests should be kept under wraps.

A woman who was a vice president came from a family of immigrants. When she talked about her cousin in Poland who was trying to come to the United States or her niece who was a cleaning lady in Brooklyn, people got uncomfortable. When it comes to interests, sometimes it's best to stick to middle-class Americana. Model cars—that's good. Collecting adult movies—that isn't.

INTERESTS AS BACKUP CAREERS

Former actress Jane Fonda was able to leverage an interest in physical fitness into a successful business. U.S. representative Carolyn McCarthy of New York's 4th District was able to turn her activism into a political career after her husband was murdered and her son injured on the Long Island Railroad. In Ohio, Patrick Swarm has turned his love for horses into a business providing riding lessons. Swarm admits that in the back of his mind he had always kept the possibility that his passion for riding could make money.[6]

Many middle-aged women have been able to turn their knowledge of houses and interior decorating into successful careers in real estate. For them, real estate was usually a second or third career to replace careers such as teaching and nursing, in which there is high burnout.

Volunteers have been able to leverage their skills into full-time jobs. After some time volunteering for *Mothers Against Drunk Drivers* (MADD), a number of women got jobs in communications. MADD provides wonderful training in public relations.

Hobbies can also be a chance to test the waters before jumping into a new career. A fifty-year-old woman was tired of working in an office. She volunteered at the local animal rescue organization to find out if she really would enjoy working with animals. She did, and went on to get a masters' degree in animal behavior. Another volunteer went on to get training in dog grooming and set up two grooming businesses.

FINDING INTERESTS

A vendor I often use was such a worker bee that she was clueless about how to develop interests. I suggested that she start out with the listings of activities in the local newspaper and *New York* magazine. That didn't work. Since she had no real passion for any of the activities she selected, she quickly dropped out. She had better luck going to a large nonprofit organization to volunteer. They carefully screened her interests, and she's now a literacy volunteer considering starting a tutoring service on the Internet. I may lose a vendor.

Some newcomers to the world of hobbies deliberately choose interests that can lead to revenue-making pursuits. It's a fairly painless way to learn about a new field. One man was approaching sixty and recognized that his days of being a full-time corporate employee would soon end. While he still had a day job, he prepared for his next career as a motivational speaker by giving talks on positive thinking at senior citizen centers. He made a strong start and went on to pursue a speaking career full time.

Now You Know...

- In high school they told us to engage in extracurricular activities. That's even more true now that we're forty, fifty, or older. Employers want to know that we're still engaged in life.
- Outside interests build bonds. They're an entree to networking and can also train us in leadership skills.
- Families are a gold mine of activities.
- Offbeat activities can alienate some.
- Hobbies can lead to careers.

12

MENTORS, AT ANY AGE

One of the oldest forms of mentoring is the family. Several generations of family members would sit around the dinner table and comment on our performance. They'd suggest ways we could improve.

—Martin Edelston, founder and president of Boardroom, Inc.

What Do I Do?

- At fifty-three I sense the powers that be are planning to eliminate my job.
- At forty-five I have a hunch that it would be a waste of time to get an MBA.
- I've been hearing that Company X hires older people. Should I present myself as the solid "voice of experience" or as a "dynamic tiger"?

MENTORS MEAN HELP AT ANY AGE

Find a mentor. It might sound strange for people over forty to think about using mentors. At our age, we're supposed to have the game down cold, right? Wrong.

The *Wall Street Journal* instituted a career column because we're all having so many questions about what to do. *Fortune* magazine has cover stories warning us that it's an entirely new game and we better learn the

165

new rules. We're hiring psychologists to accompany us to our meetings and to sit in our offices and observe. They're telling us whether we're seeing things right or are paranoid. Personal coaches are helping us gain a competitive advantage. And most of us fear that tap on the shoulder that will put us out of the game—at least for a while.

Mentors have become as necessary as Windows operating systems and plenty of exercise. They give us advice. Call it a second opinion on what we should or should not be doing. Every six months, I call a man in Chicago and run my ideas about personnel changes in the office by him. Do I call him my mentor? No, but he serves the same function. He knows me. He knows my office. He sees things I don't. At Boardroom, Inc., publisher of the newsletter *Bottom Line*, *Tax Hotline*, and *Moneysworth*, the president, Martin Edelston, has a "buddy," or universal mentoring, system. Everyone who joins Boardroom has a "buddy," who answers all sorts of questions. Turnover is low at Boardroom, and there are few personnel problems. Getting the right advice can make a big difference in individual careers and organizations.

Mentors can also open doors for us. If there's a promotion in the wings at the office, mentors can speak on our behalf. Often mentors introduce us to people who can help us. There was a shy but brilliant professor of English who was looking for a new job. His mentor took him to meet dozens of contacts at the Modern Language Association annual meeting. At conferences around the world, there is usually someone there who will see to it that I get to know the right people. I sometimes joke and think of this individual as my guardian angel.

Mentors often show us how to do our jobs. In my office I have a technology mentor who helps me convert my e-mail attachments into the software of the firm. For a writer, a good editor is an invaluable mentor. For psychotherapists, a supervisor can see problems in the case and recommend a change in the treatment plan. For those of us in our second, third, or fourth career, we may already have had mentors teach us our new jobs, and they might have been younger than us.

I wonder if the former CEO of Sunbeam, Al Dunlap, had had a mentor, he might still be in his job today. A mentor could have called to his attention that cost cutting is only one strategy to improve the bottom line. Another important strategy is building the business.

In return for their help, we give our "buddy," "guardian angel," or mentor loyalty. They may also call upon us to give them advice. We might know people they don't and may be able to open doors for them. Sometimes we assist them with their jobs. A fifty-year-old man was studying for a doctoral degree in psychology. Occasionally he taught his mentor's classes when the mentor was traveling.

MENTORS IN ALL SORTS OF PACKAGES

The classic mentor configuration used to be older mentor, younger protégé. That's no longer so pervasive.

Older mentors, if they're still working, probably don't have the time to deal with us—it's a global economy for them, too. We're seeing more and more older mentors protecting their time and saying no when we ask them for ten minutes. Also, some of the older mentors we've looked to in the past may have become out-of-date. In a global economy, things happen so fast that if executives are focused inward on a crisis for a few months they could be missing the big picture outside their companies.

THE OLD GUARD

If older executives do have the time and are in touch with current realities, they could be a gold mine, with the power, connections, and a track record for survival. We should continue to nurture relationships with them. We can keep the relationship alive by reminding them that we still exist. If they are giving a speech in town we should attend, congratulate them afterward, and send them a follow-up letter with our insights about the speech. We should join organizations to which they belong, such as the Business Roundtable. If we publish a book or an article, we should send them a copy. We can volunteer to help them out with their work.

How do we attract an older mentor? In *The Mentor Connection*, Michael Zey says that potential mentors want their protégés to be bright, loyal, ambitious, willing to deal with power and risk, able to perform the mentor's job, politically astute, positive, able to work well with others, and share the mentor's opinions about work.

I've found that old-fashioned types of communication, such as "snail mail," gets the attention of a potential older mentor. If there's an article about them in *Forbes*, we can send a note with some interesting observations. We can also attract their attention if *we're* the ones mentioned in the news. Often we get a note from them saying they would like to meet us.

If we don't personally know members of the old guard, they we can read their books or read about them. One article by Peter Drucker on contracting-out work gave me entirely new insights on how I should be running my business. Although I don't know international expert Kenichi Ohmae, I follow his thinking on the global marketplace. Increasingly, however, we'll be finding our mentors among our peers, people younger than we are, our families, and "dead thinkers" such as Shakespeare.

PEER MENTORS

If we're having trouble with the new manager at the office, often a good person to talk with is a colleague or professional friend who has known us for years. They really understand how we're "wired," and they know enough about our organization to have a fix on its political dynamics.

It's also possible to get help from a new acquaintance, especially if they have specialized knowledge. We might need to find out how to present ourselves to an executive recruiter. Say we meet Chris, an executive recruiter, at a party. We can call him and ask for ten minutes of his time, drop our problem in his lap, and take or leave his advice. With peer mentoring there aren't as many hurt feelings as there are with older mentors. Our peers see us as equals and as capable of making our own decision after we get their advice. Peers are also more approachable. I have no trouble asking a peer to introduce me to his boss. I can call up a peer at 10:00 P.M. and pour my heart out.

When our problem is resolved, we probably won't talk with our peer mentor in depth until the next problem appears—ours or theirs. At this stage of our career we shouldn't be meeting with a mentor every week, and we should have a number of different types of mentors whom we can call. One might be an expert in computers. Another might know a lot of people in our field. One might be brilliant in office politics. Still another might know how to dress.

In return for helping us, the peer mentor eventually will feel free to ask us a favor, which might be that we drop everything and give them advice on short notice, or introduce them to our superior. I've returned many favors by providing information that a peer mentor needs.

The time to lay the groundwork for a peer mentoring relationship is *before* we need it. Make friends while everything is going fine; then you'll make a good impression. In *Black Enterprise* magazine, Dawn Baskerville advises us to reach out to a potential mentor from a position of strength, not weakness. "No one," says Baskerville, "leaps to the aid of a whiner."[2] When we're networking, we have to keep our eyes open for peers in whom we might want to confide when the chips are down or when we're confused. We can ask around to find out if they're discreet.

YOUTH

Many mentors are now younger than we are. That's because more and more of our superiors and clients are younger than we are. From younger people, we can learn everything from the latest software to what alternative life styles are now in vogue. The House of Windsor might not be so threatened today if Queen Elizabeth II had accepted some young mentors in the palace. Her late daughter-in-law, Diana, would have been ideal. Without coaching from younger people, almost everything became dated about the House of Windsor, from how they express emotion to their understanding of the global economy.

When Karen Ritchie set out to research and write her book *Marketing to Generation X*, she first talked to the young clerk in the mailroom. That's how Ritchie got her direction. After losing substantial market share, Levi Strauss belatedly sent a young networker into the inner city to try to learn what trends are emerging and what younger urban people want their jeans to look like. Levi Strauss missed out on the wide-body look.

We can attract the interest of younger people if we're sincere in wanting their input. It's very obvious if we're insincere when talking about a musical group or various "zines." We can break the ice by having a copy of *Wired* or *Details* on our desk. Or we can ask the younger people what they thought of a certain article. We can join gyms where younger people work out. In most communities the folks who go to bars are younger people. We can meet them there. We can ask friends to introduce us to their children, or hire younger people and informally use them as mentors. We can volunteer for a political campaign. Those attract lots of younger people.

In return for their help, we have plenty to give our young mentors. We have experience. For example, we can explain to them which bosses not to work for. We have contacts, and unique sources of information.

FAMILIES

As Martin Edelston said in the beginning quotation, families have always been a good source for mentoring. An article in *Newsweek* presents famous people, ranging from Michael Jordan to Cokie Roberts, who see a family member as being their primary mentor.[4] When fathers began to mentor daughters, there was a surge in the number of women going after top jobs.

Families are ideal settings for mentoring because there is a mix of generations, and wisdom comes from all ages. When a grandfather in the retail business for thirty years and a grandson at a fashion institute slug it out, you're going to learn something.

One part of the family we usually neglect to seek for advice is our own children. In the digital age, they can be incredibly helpful. One look from my twelve-year-old son when I'm on the phone with a client lets me know that I'm going about the task like an "old man." He lets me know when the language I use is anachronistic and he's educated me about all the latest musical developments.

One advantage of being mentored by your children is that the process is private. You can be as stupid as you really are about technology or mountain climbing.

OURSELVES

Another source of mentoring is ourselves. Edelston says that we are often our own best mentor since we know ourselves and our situation so well. All we have to do is reach inside and gain access to our inner wisdom. Denis Boyles in *Success* agrees. He believes that being

mentored should culminate in our being able to mentor ourselves—
and others.[5] To illustrate, after we have been through three restruc-
turings, we can pretty well mentor ourselves on the moves we should
be making. We can ask ourselves: "What did I do in the last
restructuring that saved my job? What are the pitfalls during a
restructuring? How low a profile should I keep? What's the worst-case
scenario of what can happen?"

To tap into this mentor within, we need to have confidence in our
instincts. That shouldn't be hard, since we have plenty of experience
and a track record for success. If we lack this confidence, the quickest
way to get it is to mentor others; then we will realize how much we
know. Every community has a literacy program where we can teach
people how to read, or to speak English as a second language.

DEAD MENTORS

Edelston also recommends that we reach back into the past for
mentoring. His favorite "dead mentors" include Dale Carnegie and
Napoleon Hill, the noted motivational authority, who wrote the bestselling *Think and Grow Rich*. My favorite is Shakespeare; his history
plays provide a Ph.D. in politics, and using history as a guide helps
reassure us that our problems aren't unique. There was a time in
corporate America when executives were studying the great books of
the Western world as a way to gain perspective on current management problems.

Negative learning is also useful. If we read the biography of Henry
Ford, we know how Ford got carried away and assumed he was an
expert on nonautomotive matters, such as world politics. He also
almost lost his shirt because he initially resisted innovations such as
new models, new colors (black was king for Ford), and the concept of
planned obsolescence.

DOWNSIDE OF MENTORING

The goodies of mentoring don't come risk free; there can be a
downside. One of the most common problems is outgrowing our
mentors. Joe might have been useful to us when we were first starting
our business, but now he's an albatross who always calls. Mary might
have been helpful to us when we were job hunting, but now that we're

back at work she's no use in helping us survive politically. How do we get rid of mentors?

The challenge is to become more independent without hurting their feelings or threatening their power. Sometimes all this requires is common sense, but other times it's more difficult. Frequently, the president or number-two person in a company will outgrow the CEO who was once his mentor. In those situations it's not unusual for the former protégé to be kicked out of the company. Powerful mentors can treat us like slaves.

It also works the other way. Protégés can do in mentors. David Batchelder, cofounder of Relational Investors L.P., helped bring down his mentor, T. Boone Pickins, former chairman of Mesa, Inc.[6] A number of Lee Iacocca's former protégés eventually turned on him.

As Michael Zey points out in *The Mentor Connection*, there are myriad other ways that a mentor-protégé relationship can go sour. The mentor may fall from grace, and that will reflect back badly on the protégé. The mentor may get a big promotion and not want to be bothered with the protégé anymore. Or the protégé may rise in the organization higher than the mentor and may find more powerful people interested in helping, and then wish to dump the mentor.[7]

Being mentored is so crucial in our development and during career transitions that it's worth the downside. There are points in our career—a layoff, promotion, or the beginning of self-employment—when we usually can't go it alone. I would never have attempted starting my business had I not had a number of entrepreneurial mentors guiding me. Did some of them give me advice that wasn't helpful? Sure. But their collective experience was what I needed. As the protégé, it was my responsibility to sort out what was valuable from what was off-the-wall.

NOT SO GENTLE

I think that mentoring got the image of being warm and fuzzy when it evolved into formal programs in companies. Senior executives, it was believed, would tell their protégés how much potential they had, and that they only had to take a few courses to bring it out. The advice was supposedly nice and supportive.

But mentoring doesn't necessarily mean gentle nurturance. In these volatile times, most of the mentors I've encountered were pretty blunt with me. If they thought I was moving too slowly, they shouted at me to get the lead out of my pants. Candice Carpenter, CEO of iVillage, uses "radical mentoring." According to *Fast Company*, Carpenter pushes the protégé faster than they might want to grow. At the time the protégé might not be too happy to be forced to stretch, but the end result is usually wonderful.[8]

Mentoring has rarely been peaches and cream. Mentors can be brutal. One of my early editors called me in and asked, "Bob, is your native language English?" I told him it was. He then asked me why I wasn't writing in English. That was the last time I used a grandiose style of writing. Not too long ago, I had lunch with one of my mentors. She's twenty-five, and she told me that I was thinking in clichés.

In this economic environment we've got to have a tough skin to work with mentors.

JAMES SCOFIELD O'ROURKE, IV

Notre Dame, my alma mater, is known for its mentoring of students. Therefore, I asked James Scofield O'Rourke, IV, Ph.D., to give us his perspective on mentoring.

Dr. O'Rourke is director of the Eugene D. Fanning Center for Business Communication at Notre Dame and a consultant to *Fortune* 500 companies as well as midsize businesses. O'Rourke teaches writing and speaking at Notre Dame and is widely published. In his twenty-nine-year career, he has earned an international reputation in business communication. *Business Week* named him one of the "outstanding faculty" in Notre Dame's graduate business school.

* * *

INTERVIEW WITH JAMES SCOFIELD O'ROURKE, IV

RD: We have been hearing a lot about the importance of mentors in the last ten years or so. Why?

JO: There are two reasons for this. One, the increasing instability in the workforce has forced people to think beyond their expertise, their education, and their experience. Many people now find themselves in jobs and organizations that they would never have dreamed of joining just a few years ago.

Second, we are experiencing accelerating rates of change. Things have always changed, but at a much slower rate. Today, everything from workplace technology to product cycles have accelerated and shortened. You don't have a week to think this over; your team chief needs an answer this morning. Who do you turn to for advice? In the past, many of us would have gone directly to our supervisors. Today, the supervisor may not even be on-site. If she is, she's probably in a meeting or dealing with some other crisis. A mentor may have your best answers.

RD: I know what you mean, Jim. When I select a mentor it has to be someone I can gain access to right away. Is it common now to have more than one mentor?

JO: It's not only common, it's probably essential. One person can't know all aspects of the job. For instance, you might turn to one person you trust for technical advice, knowing that he'll provide current, accurate information you can rely on. He also won't reveal how little you know to others in the organization.

And then, you might turn to another person you trust for political advice. Of course, this is the most sensitive and most difficult sort of advice to find. Good political advisors can give you a feel for which move might be good and which might be dangerous. They can review numerous hypothetical situations with you, all in advance of your actual decision.

RD: Can older workers benefit from having younger mentors?

JO: As workers age, the danger is that they will continue to rely on what's always worked for them, but as technology advances, relationships change, and the economic landscape shifts, an older worker might very well benefit from having younger friends to rely on. The trick, of course, is establishing a two-way relationship with someone you can trust—someone who won't betray your confidence and who really does know what he's talking about. A younger mentor can help prevent your skills from becoming dated and can give you a sense of being in touch with what's happening now, rather than what happened when you were first making a name for yourself.

RD: How does an older worker attract a younger mentor? What's in it for a younger worker?

JO: That's a difficult question. Often, it's a matter of personal chemistry. Frequently, an older worker can attract a younger mentor simply by walking into her office and asking a couple of job-related questions. Let's say you're preparing for a talk to a group of overseas customers next week and would like to upgrade the quality of your presentation graphics. Asking a techno-savvy young manager a few direct questions about building a PowerPoint presentation would give that manager an opportunity to show you what she knows. It's a great chance to learn.

Another way to make friends with younger workers is simply to find people with similar or common interests. They might be anything from sports or hobbies to current events. You might even look for younger men and women at the college you attended. A link to your old alma mater is a great way to build a relationship.

In exchange, of course, it's always useful if you can provide something that younger managers can take to the bank. You might be able to provide advice on the culture of your organizations or its informal workings, or perhaps some counsel on why certain projects and programs succeeded or failed in the past.

RD: I think the key word is *trust*. We must be able to trust the younger manager. One woman in her fifties got a job in a New Jersey telecommunications firm, and proclaimed more expertise with a certain software than she had. Several times she asked a younger manager for help with it, and he let everyone in the office know that she had misrepresented her skills. For that reason, is it sometimes more advisable to seek help from younger people away from the workplace? Wouldn't that protect privacy?

JO: It's a good idea to have multiple mentors, and, if you can, find one away from the workplace who can provide specific kinds of advice that could be useful. Having someone you can speak with in confidence may be essential. Off-site mentors are sometimes difficult to connect with, though. Also, they might not know much about your specific organization. Keep in mind that as you age, it's essential that you develop friendships of all ages, all occupations, and as many of them in as many locations as possible.

RD: Can older workers benefit from having mentors their age? I have several of these.

JO: You're really talking about peer mentoring here. And, yes, developing solid reciprocal relationships with peers is crucial to your success, both in the short term and over the long haul. Peers know precisely what you're going through at each stage of your career. They know the emotional as well as the cognitive experiences you're confronting. They can often provide advice on areas of work-life balance that you're reluctant to talk about with others in the organization, particularly those who have yet to face or haven't recently faced the problems you're confronting.

RD: For just those reasons, peer mentoring is going to become big. Talking with my peers is "safer" than talking to others in that my peers know what I'm going through. We can also talk in shorthand. On the downside of mentoring, what are the risks involved?

JO: There can be several disadvantages. The first is that you may rely too much on your mentor's advice and not think through the issues and options for yourself. Remember, a mentor is very much like a teacher or a coach. He or she is there to help you learn, grow, and develop as a manager and a leader. You don't want to rely on her so extensively that you fail to develop the skills or instincts that you'll need in the months and years ahead.

Second, you may select the wrong mentor. It happens for a variety of reasons. You may be attracted to a person because of his, or her, success or because of a specific skill set, but that particular mentor may be wrong for you.

For instance, many years ago I selected as my mentor a successful field grade officer in the air force. He was insightful, articulate, bright, and very well connected. Since I was just emerging from the junior ranks, he looked wonderful to me. As I tried to learn the culture and pitfalls of a new organization, he turned out to be helpful in many ways. The problem was that he was misusing the relationship. As he asked me to participate in projects and activities he was either directing or involved in, I found great opportunities to grow. Before long, however, I discovered that I was doing a lot of his work. After a year's time and a half-dozen projects, I calculated that another young officer and I were doing nearly a third of the mentor's work. My own work began to suffer, and the hours I was putting in were unbelievable.

You may also select the wrong mentor, perhaps because you're simply naive. You may find a senior official who befriends you but who can't really tell you or show you anything you need to know. He may not have the time to devote to conversation, counseling, or instruction. Or, you may select someone who is politically out of favor in the organization. You could get dragged into politics that would damage you over the long term.

Another problem with mentoring is that it can be misconstrued. If people of the opposite sex are mentoring each other, they have to be aware of what others may be saying. Appearances matter in every organization. While I don't discourage such relationships, I advise mentors and protégés to be professional in their dealings. They should consider how their actions appear. A personal gesture could be interpreted as romance, not mentoring. Keep everything, including titles and gestures, professional.

RD: What are the red flags that a mentoring relationship is running into trouble?

JO: I see several. First, if a mentor simply doesn't have the time that the protégé needs, then the two of them should acknowledge that this relationship may not be in the best interest of the junior member. Second, if a mentor begins to involve the protégé in inappropriate activities or work relationships that are not purely beneficial to the junior member, it may be time to step back and examine the relationship. Finally, if a mentor is nearing the end of a career or a career phase involving a number of changes, then both the mentor and the protégé may wish to think about how and whether to continue the relationship.

RD: Can someone repair a mentoring relationship? I've seen mentoring relationships in corporate life start to go downhill and no one seems to know what to do to fix them.

JO: The more important question to ask is why someone has chosen a mentoring relationship in the first place. From the protégé's point of view, what do you hope to gain or learn? From the mentor's point of view, what do you know that you can share? All mentoring relationships should be seen from an objective perspective.

People who need help should seek it from the right person. Once that particular type of help is no longer needed, it's usually wise to draw back from the relationship. Check in now and then. Remain friends. But don't invest the same time or energy.

There are other types of mentoring relationships in which the original goals are accomplished, but both a mentor and protégé want to continue working together. That's fine, but to prevent problems, it's important to specify the new goals. This is how smart people in organizations handle some of the transitions in mentoring relationships. Always keep the objectives clear.

Approaching mentoring relationships strategically can prevent problems down the road. If a relationship starts to unravel, go back and review your original objectives.

RD: What do you tell the students at Notre Dame about the importance of a mentor?

JO: I tell students that they can succeed without one but that life will be easier, less stressful, and more fun with one or more appropriate mentors. I tell them to find someone in their new organizations whom they admire, someone who knows the business, its products, services, and technology. I tell them to connect with people who seem best skilled at the very things they most need to know. I encourage them to ask around, check the political standing or reputation of those they're considering. Go slowly. I also tell them to be wary of people who "volunteer" to take you under their wing. In addition, I emphasize the importance of personal chemistry in a mentoring relationship.

Both people must enjoy the time they spend together.

RD: Do you have mentors right now?

JO: Certainly. I take on new mentors to help me in new roles that I'm called upon to play and new responsibilities that I'm assigned to. I stay in touch with old mentors, but often they hear from me just once or twice a year. Today when I have a question or a problem, I'll ask one of my newer mentors for a few minutes on the phone; sometimes we'll get together for lunch or attend a social event.

One of the most inspiring and helpful mentors I've had in thirty years of professional and academic life was a man named Gene Fanning. He was an investor, a sports franchise owner, and, before that, an automobile dealer in Chicago. Gene was a prince of a guy, always available to talk, always ready to listen, and always there to help me work my way through a problem. The fact that he's gone now doesn't diminish his influence on my life. I still ask myself from time to time: What would Gene do in this situation? How would he respond? How would he handle this? The answers to those questions are invariably useful as I grapple with the latest crisis on my desk.

* * *

USING MENTORS EFFECTIVELY

From what Jim O'Rourke has said about the mentor relationship, it's clear that we have to know what we want when we go into the relationship. Otherwise, we could be disappointed and even abused. At this stage of our work life, what is it that we want? Here are some of the things I'm looking for from my various mentors:

- Guidance on how to stay employable—what companies do I have to make now to keep at the top of my game?
- Advice on what I might be doing or saying to come across as "old."
- Training in new skill. (Perhaps a mentor can teach me how to write for the Internet.)
- Discussion of new perspectives. (If we use performance reviews, does that mean that we're not doing our management job all year?)
- Advice on how to still put in a fourteen-hour day and not get exhausted.
- Insights on getting new clients.
- Providing leadership in the office, including motivating young employees.

When I have achieved my goal, then, as O'Rourke said, it's time to stand back and see if it's useful to continue the relationship at the same intensity. After all mentoring relationships aren't friendships per se.

They can grow into friendships, but that's not their primary purpose. If I want to continue with the relationship, then it's time to draw up a new set of objectives. This can all be done informally, but it should be done. When mentoring relations drift, it's usually the protégé who winds up with the short end of the stick.

Now You Know...

- No matter what our age, we need mentoring.
- Mentors are a multipurpose tool.
- More and more of our mentoring will come from peers, young people, families, ourselves, and figures from history.
- There's a downside to mentoring, but the process is so crucial that we should seek out mentoring anyway.
- Approach mentoring strategically. Formulate objectives. Monitor how things are going.

13

CONCLUSION

ALL OVER THE PLACE

Today, the trick to being an older worker is to accept that your career might not be what you thought it was going to be. Instead of being linear, your career may be all over the place. Maybe you don't have as many options. You might have five clients, teach two courses in communications as an adjunct professor at a university, and be training to be a financial planner, but certain avenues have been closed to you.

GETTING THE HANG OF IT

Once we accept that we'll be on a roller coaster, earning a living and enjoying ourselves, life should become more manageable. Actually, once we've come through the first few career shocks, future career crises won't seem so shocking. Thanks to career shocks, we're stronger, wiser, and more resilient. We know now to get away from drudge work and push for assignments that will teach us new skills and put us in touch with useful people. We understand that balance means survival and that we will continue to survive no matter how intense or rewarding work gets. And we've become philosophical about getting or losing an assignment or a job. They come and they go. So what. We only have to worry if they're going too often and too unexpectedly. Then we should look at all our systems and figure out which ones should be working better.

LATE BLOOMERS

A number of us, as Ken Dychtwald said, will become late bloomers. I've seen how it's easier for older workers to hit those home runs more effortlessly than when they were younger. We know more. We know how to handle ourselves. Older workers tend to be less self-conscious and self-absorbed than younger workers and can keep their focus totally on an assignment. One media representative who's seventy-one got about forty top national reporters to show up for a press conference with an economist. The press room looked so packed that it could have been the White House. And the coverage was positive. I don't think the rep could have pulled off that coup thirty years ago. Back then, his mind was on himself and what was going on at home and in the office. Today, this man is a tiger because he isn't distracted.

Late blooming for us might take the form of a second or third career. A man left the acting profession and in his late forties became a psychotherapist. He's much more successful—and fulfilled—in his second profession than he was in his first. A woman I work with is exploring getting a master's degree in animal behavior. At fifty-three, she feels that she's too "old" to become a veterinarian but still wants the credentials to be in a profession involved with animals. Since she is also a published author, she could make a big splash writing about animals.

POWER

With aging also comes new forms of power. In *The Power Game*, journalist Hedrick Smith dissected all the ways he can possess power. Visibility is power. Access is power. Many of us older professionals have these types of power—in spades.[1] As Dychtwald also pointed out, our sheer numbers are giving us clout in shaping public policies. The AARP is one of the most effective lobbying groups in the nation.

PERSPECTIVE

Being older also means that we probably have survived everything from a reorganization to the moment when the consultants march in, which means that we have perspective. If we make ourselves available as mentors to younger people, that generation will help us keep up to speed on trends.

KEEPING MENTALLY, PHYSICALLY, AND SPIRITUALLY SOUND

What do we have to do to keep in cognitive, physical, and spiritual shape for the roller-coaster ride? I have some suggestions.

- Tell what you know. In the magazine *George*, Gretchen Craft Rubin wrote that the way to get to be a valuable commodity is to let people know that you know.[2] Before I answer the phone or go out the door, I make sure that I have some information on everything from baseball and politics to the layoffs on Wall Street and the latest in human genome science in my head. In transmitting information, age is a plus. We have decades and decades of contacts feeding us information.

- Assume that the career track we're on is going to fizzle out. Maybe it'll be less in demand; maybe the money won't be there anymore; or maybe we'll burn out. Speechwriting used to be a secure job in corporate America, but about 1985, more and more speeches started to be outsourced. Alert speechwriters prepared for this by learning other skills, such as dealing with the media or handling investor relations.

- No matter how heady an experience, or fulfilling, work is, we've got to keep trying to hang on to a life. When a career shock comes, often it's our real-life contacts that help us through, not our professional associations. Make it a practice that no matter what is happening at the office, at work, or in your office at home, leave at a certain time each day. Staying glued to work will kill you.

- Since health is a prerequisite to work, you have to spend time seeing the appropriate round of doctors, dentists, and healers. I knew one busy executive who went several years without a physical. Then, one day, sixty pounds overweight, he had the big one. Work is never worth your health.

- Volunteer work is nature's cure-all for everything from ennui to feeling under-appreciated. Executives probably feel better about their pro bono work than they do about what's paying the mortgage. Volunteer activity often leads to board positions—and that's a gold mine for networking.

- If we're becoming detached at work, maybe it's time to either recommit ourselves or find something else to do. Since our careers are now so long, it's easy to burn out several times. One good way to recharge our batteries is to take a sabbatical. If we go through the want ads from beginning 'til end, we're apt to find other ways to make a living.

- In many professions, work has become the night of the long knives, but if we understand why people are trying to do us in, we won't become bitter and dysfunctional. A client used to call me with an assignment on Fridays at 3:00 P.M. Then, on Monday mornings he would complain to his boss that I hadn't done it. I could have hated this man, but I forgave him because I could see that he was using me to try to survive. He could no longer win in the game on his own steam. In fact, today he is out of the game.

- We have to be our own public relations agency. We've got to tell people about our accomplishments—on the train to work, on phone calls, on e-mail, at lunches, and through newsletters. That's layer number one of public relations. Layer number two is media coverage, including appearing on television and radio. Layer number three is a book. A book is a multidimensional public relations tool. Books put Al Ries and Jack Trout on the map. A book made Stephen Covey the spiritual guru for business.

- Select areas in which to remain an expert—and declare, then and there, that enough is enough. Limits have to be set since the pool of information is almost limitless today and continually expanding. We can't be retrieving and processing data all day. Many on-line services will flag us on the basis of category about what we should be reading or watching. And after we ingest that material, we should go out to play tennis.

HOW LUCKY WE ARE

There have been those among us—John F. Kennedy, Martin Luther King, Jr., and Princess Diana—who never had the opportunity to grow older. Well, we do have that opportunity. For many of us that means twenty, thirty, or forty more years of work. What we can accomplish in that time! As conservative Barry Goldwater aged, he saw his ideology being embraced and enshrined during the twelve-year Reagan-Bush reign and reinforced by President Clinton, who has been called the "most conservative Democratic president of the twentieth century." Madonna could create something totally new during the second half of her career. As he hits fifty, Prince Charles is becoming a person in his own right with an enhanced public image as a devoted father to his two young sons following Princess Diana's tragic death. The scientist Friedrich Alexander von Humbolt produced his landmark work, *The Kosmos*, in his seventy-sixth year.

So there are a few bumps in the road, a few things we forget, a few employers who don't want anything to do with us. But the bottom line is that these extra years are a gift to us. Use them well.

NOTES

Introduction

1. Tony Horwitz, "Some Who Lost Jobs Early in the Nineties Recession Find Hard Road Back," *Wall Street Journal*, June 26, 1998, Al.

2. Linda Thornburg, "The Age Wave Hits," *HR Magazine*, February 1995, 40.

3. Robert Lewis, "Boomers to Reinvent Retirement," *AARP Bulletin*, June 1998, 1, 16–17.

4. Tom Wolfe, *A Man in Full* (New York: Farrar Straus Giroux, 1998).

5. Wolfe, 78.

6. "Study: Students Biased Against Older Workers," *Nation's Restaurant News*, November 8, 1993, 34.

7. Letty Cottin Pogrebin, *Getting Over Getting Older* (Boston: Little, Brown, 1996).

8. Betty Friedan, *The Fountain of Age* (New York: Simon and Schuster, 1993).

9. Andrew Sullivan, "Status in a Class-Free Society," *New York Times Magazine*, November 15, 1998.

Chapter 1. Why We Come Across as "Old"

1. James Medoff, "Why Business is Axing Older Workers," *U.S. News & World Report*, Oct 31, 1994, 78.

2. "Once Secure Workers Now Face 'Survival of the Fittest,'" http://www.usatoday.com/news/index/down/down0.1.htm.

3. "Older Workers Into the New Millennium," Senior Employment Program, http://www.sremploy.org/olderw.html.

4. Andrew E. Scharlach and Lenard Kaye, eds., *Controversial Issues in Aging* (Boston: Allyn and Bacon, 1997).

5. "Successful Aging," *Publishers Weekly*, February 1998, 86.

Chapter 2. Bosses

1. Betty Friedan, *The Fountain of Age* (New York: Simon and Schuster, 1993).

2. Robert Atchley, Ph.D., "Is Gerontology Biased Toward a Negative View of the Aging Process and Old Age?" *Controversial Issues in Aging*, ed.

Andrew E. Scharlach and Lenard Kaye (Boston: Allyn and Bacon, 1997), 185–96.

3. Carol Kymowitz, "Young Managers Learn How to Bridge the Gap With Older Employees," *Wall Street Journal*, July 21, 1998, B1.

4. Robert Lewis, "Boomers to Reinvent Retirement," *AARP Bulletin*, June 1998, 1, 16–17.

5. Jeffrey Tannenbaum, "Retiree Lesson: A Couple's Solution to Money and Work," *Wall Street Journal*, October 13, 1998, B2.

6. "Dissecting Success," *Wall Street Journal*, October 15, 1998, A1.

Chapter 3. Free Agents Can Finish First

1. Alan Webber, "Show Me the Money!" *Fast Company*, November 1998, 198.

2. Reed Abelson, "Part-Time Work for Some Adds Up to Full-Time Work," *New York Times*, November 2, 1998, A1.

3. Daniel Pink, "The Talent Market," *Fast Company*, August 1998, 88.

4. Warren Bennis and Burt Nanus, *Leaders* (New York: Harper and Row, 1985).

5. Charles Handy, *The Age of Unreason* (Boston: Harvard Business School Press, 1989) 87–117.

6. Pink, 100, 102.

Chapter 4. Bouncing Back From a Setback

1. John Ward, *Song of the Phoenix: The Hidden Rewards of Failure* (Stockbridge, Mass.: Berkshire House, 1992), 50.

2. Katharine Graham, *Personal History* (New York: Vantige Books, 1997), 339–625.

3. Hedrick Smith, *The Power Game* (New York: Random House, 1988).

4. Dale Carnegie, *How to Win Friends and Influence People* (New York: Simon and Schuster, 1936).

5. Peter Drucker, "New Paradigms," *Forbes*, October 5, 1998, 152–179.

Chapter 5. When Our Values Change

1. Harriet Rubin, "Success and Excess," *Fast Company*, October 1998, 110–128.

2. Charles Handy, *The Hungry Spirit* (New York: Broadway Books, 1998).

3. Gail Sheehy, *New Passages* (New York: Ballantine Books, 1995).

4. John Sculley, *Odyssey* (New York: Harper and Row, 1988).

5. Joan Lloyd, "What Motivates You," http://www.connectme.com/articles/joanlloyd/What—motivates-you.html.

6. Caroline Myss, Ph.D., *Why People Don't Heal* (New York: Three Rivers Press, 1997), 3–28.

7. Sandra Blakeslee, "Placebos Prove So Powerful Even Experts Are Surprised," *New York Times*, October 13, 1998, 1, 4.

8. Myss, 98–100.

Chapter 6. Staying "Smart"

1. Joseph Nocera, "Charting a New Course," *Fortune*, August 17, 1998, 75.

2. Jean-Claude Paye, "Strategies for a Learning Society," *OECD Observer*, April–May 1996, 4–6.

3. Donald Robinson and Timothy Galpin, "In for a Change," *HR Magazine*, July 1996, 90–94.

4. Peter M. Senge, *The Fifth Discipline: The Art and Practice of the Learning Organization* (New York: Doubleday Currency, 1990).

5. Lawrence Brandon, "Learning Organizations Hold the Key to Success," *National Underwriter Property and Casualty-Risk and Benefits Management*, October 25, 1993, 22–24.

6. Howard Gardner, *Frames of Mind: The Theory of Multiple Intelligences*, 10th anniversary edition (New York: Basic Books, 1993).

7. Charles Fishman, "The War for Talent," *Fast Company*, August 1998, 104.

8. Leonard Hayflick, Ph.D., *How and Why We Age* (New York: Ballantine Books, 1994), 142–143.

9. Sarah Braley, "Golden Tools," *Meetings and Conventions*, June 1998, 77–81.

Chapter 7. Networking—Building Social Capital After Forty

1. Donna Fenn, "A League of Your Own," *Inc.*, May 19, 1998, 102–108.

2. Robert Ramsey, "Networking in the Nineties," *Supervision*, May 1997, 9–13.

3. Steven Ginsberg, "For More Workers, It's a Smooze," *Washington Post*, October 12, 1997, H2.

4. Phil Agre, "Networking on the Network," *Crossroads*, May 18, 1998, www.acm.org/crossroads/xrds4-4/network.html.

5. Agre, "Networking on the Network."

6. Fenn, "A League of Your Own."

7. Chase, "Networking."

8. Keith Davis, "Management Communication and the Grapevine," *People: Managing Your Most Important Asset* (Boston: Harvard Business Review, 1988), 84–90.

9. Terrence Deal and Allan Kennedy, *Corporate Cultures* (New York: Addison-Wesley Publishing Company, 1982), 85–106.

10. Daniel Coleman, *Emotional Intelligence* (New York: Bantam Books, 1995).

11. Michael Pratt and Joan Norris, *The Social Psychology of Aging* (Cambridge: Blackwell, 1994), 61.

Chapter 8. If It's a Job You Want

1. "Seniors Fill Job Deficit," *Industry Week*, July 6, 1998, 12.

2. Martin Yate, *Beat the Odds* (New York: Ballantine Books, 1995), 3.

3. Richard Nelson Bolles, 1999 edition, *What Color Is Your Parachute?: A Practical Manual for Job-Hunters and Career-Changers* (Ten Speed Press).

4. Peter Drucker, *Managing for the Future* (New York: Truman Talley Books, 1992), 203.

5. Thomas Petziner, Jr., "Gary Klein Studies How Our Minds Dictate Those 'Gut Feelings,'" *Wall Street Journal*, August 7, 1998, B1.

6. Erving Goffman, *The Presentation of Self in Everyday Life* (New York: Doubleday Books, 1959).

Chapter 9. Being Self-Employed

1. Diane Crispell, "The Lure of the Entrepreneur," *American Demographics*, February 1998, 40–42.

2. "Inside Track," *Success*, July 1998, 12.

3. Steven Bursten, *The Bootstrap Entrepreneur* (Nashville, Tenn.: Thomas Nelson Publishers, 1993), 25.

4. Tom Kulzer, "Profile of an Entrepreneur," *Profits On-Line*, 1996, http://www.profitsonline,com/profit.../Articles/ArticlesI-N/kilzer2.html.

5. John Case, "The Dark Side: Births and Deaths," *Inc.*, May 15, 1996, 80.

6. Mark Richard Moss, "Fourth Time's the Charm," *Nation's Business*, May 1998, 85.

7. Ralph Hass and Thom Crimas, "Former Corporate Players Look to Franchises for Self-Employment," *Austin Business Journal*, November 24, 1997, http://www.amcity.com/austin/stories/112497/focus8.html.

8. Gustav Berle, *SBA Hotline Answer Book* (New York: John Wiley and Sons, 1994), 1.

9. William Alarid and Gustave Berle, *Free Help From Uncle Sam to Start Your Own Business (or Expand the One You Have)*, 3rd ed. (Santa Maria, Calif.: Puma Publishing, 1992).

10. Robert Bly and Gary Blake, "Out on Your Own: From Corporate to

Self-Employment," *Looking for the Business of Your Dreams?*, http:/www.smartbiz.com/sbs/arts/bly66.htm.

11. "The Untouchables," *Inc.*, May 1998, 74.

12. Robert L. Dilenschneider, "Interview With George Gendron," *The Critical Fourteen Years of Your Professional Life* (Secaucus, N.J.: Carol Publishing Group, 1997), 46–47.

Chapter 10. The Past *Does* Matter — If We Know How to Handle It

1. Michael Treacy and Fred Wiersema, *The Discipline of Market Leaders* (Reading, Mass.: Addison-Wesley Publishing Company, 1995).

2. Peter Drucker, *Managing for the Future* (New York: Truman Talley Books/Dutton, 1992), 191–96.

3. Gail Sheehy, *New Passages* (New York: Ballantine Books, 1995), 71.

4. Patty Duke, *A Brilliant Madness* (New York: Bantam Books, 1992).

5. Erving Goffman, *The Presentation of Self in Everyday Life* (New York: Doubleday, 1959).

Chapter 11. Beyond Work

1. Daniel Goleman, *Emotional Intelligence* (New York: Bantam Books, 1995).

2. Eugene Gilligan, "Hobbies Span the Generation Gap," *Playthings*, October 1994, 20–23.

3. David Ross, "When an Avocation Becomes a Business," *Nation's Business*, May 1995, 8.

4. Sue Shellenbarger, "For Harried Workers, Time Off Is Not Just for Family Affairs," *Wall Street Journal*, November 11, 1998, B1.

5. Tom Wolfe, *A Man in Full* (New York: Farrar Straus Giroux, 1998).

6. Harriet Tramer, "It's Their Jobs," *Crain's Cleveland Business*, March 9, 1998, 21–22.

Chapter 12. Mentors, at Any Age

1. Michael Zey, *The Mentor Connection* (Homewood, Ill.: Jones-Irwin, 1984).

2. Dawn Baskerville, "Get a Mentor," *Black Enterprise*, May 1994, 44.

3. Karen Ritchie, *Marketing to Generation X* (New York: Lexington Books, 1995), 4–5.

4. Sharon Begley, "The Parent Trap," *Newsweek*, September 7, 1998, 58–59.

5. Denis Boyles, "Find Your Guide," *Success*, July 1998, 22.

6. Seth Lubove, "The King is Dead," *Forbes*, July 15, 1996, 64–66.

7. Michael Zey, 136–165.

8. Pamela Kruger and Katherine Mieszkowski, "Stop the Fight," *Fast Company*, September 1998, 104.

Conclusion

1. Hedrick Smith, *The Power Game* (New York: Random House, 1988).

2. Gretchen Craft Rubin, "Top Ten Ways to Win Power in D.C.," *George*, December 1998, 48.